Ray-views

Volume 1

Book Reviews by Category

Ray Foy
Arbordin Park Press

Ray-views Volume 1
Copyright (c) 2015 by Ray Foy
ALL RIGHTS RESERVED

Published by Arbordin Park Press
Columbia, South Carolina, USA
www.arbordinparkpress.net

The opinions expressed in the books reviewed in this collection are not necessarily those of this collection's author. Inclusion of, or reference to, any other written works by the essays and reviews in this collection does not constitute endorsement for those works or any opinions expressed in them. No part of this publication may be reproduced, stored in a retrieval system, or transmitted in any form or by any means without prior written permission from the author, except in brief quotations in printed or electronic reviews.

Cover design and photo by Ray Foy

Contents

FOREWORD: A BOOK OF MY BOOK REVIEWS..........................1

BEYOND THE USUAL...7

    Adventures Beyond the Body by William Buhlman.........11

    The Eagle's Gift by Carlos Castaneda................................14

    Enoch: A Bigfoot Story by Autumn Williams...................17

    The Bone Clocks by David Mitchell..................................21

    Cloud Atlas by David Mitchell..24

    The Historian by Elizabeth Kostova.................................27

    Solving the Communion Enigma by Whitley Strieber....30

    From Ray's Journal:
    There is Something Here Among Us................................33

    From Ray's Journal:
    My Issues with The Bone Clocks.......................................35

    Suggested for Further Reading..38

THE HUMAN PROBLEM...39

    Ishmael by Daniel Quinn...42

    The Story of B by Daniel Quinn..45

    My Ishmael by Daniel Quinn..48

    The Chalice & The Blade by Riane Eisler.........................52

Contents

Lord of the Flies by William Golding..................55

From Ray's Journal:
We Wait for the Denouement.......................58

From Ray's Journal:
What Happened to Us? 61

Suggested for Further Reading......................63

ON PROPHECY..65

The Essential Hopi Prophecies by John Hogue............69

The Essential Nostradamus by John Hogue................72

Kamikaze Tomorrowland by John Hogue....................75

Ten Predictions for 2015 by John Hogue.................77

Predictions for 2015-2016 by John Hogue................79

Predictions for the Last Blood Moon by John Hogue....82

Francis and the Last Pope Prophecies of St. Malachy
by John Hogue...86

From Ray's Journal:
The Future..89

Suggested for Further Reading........................91

Contents

THE DYSTOPIAN POTENTIAL..93

    For Whom the Bell Tolls by Ernest Hemingway............98

    An Unfinished Life by Robert Dallek.......................102

    To Kill a Mockingbird by Harper Lee......................105

    A Mission from God by James Meredith....................108

    The Hunger Games by Suzanne Collins.....................112

    Catching Fire by Suzanne Collins.........................115

    Mockingjay by Suzanne Collins............................117

    The Witch of Hebron by James Howard Kunstler.......120

    The Road by Cormac McCarthy..............................122

    From Ray's Journal: Visions of the Future................125

    Suggested for Further Reading............................127

INSPIRATION...129

    The Alchemist by Paulo Coelho.............................134

    The Camino by Shirley MacLaine............................137

    Life of Pi by Yann Martel...................................140

    Lost Horizon by James Hilton..............................144

    The Pilgrimage by Paulo Coelho.............................148

Contents

Man's Search for Meaning by Viktor Frankl..................150

Run by Ann Patchett..................153

State of Wonder by Ann Patchett..................156

Wild by Cheryl Strayed..................159

2001: A Space Odyssey by Arthur C. Clarke..................162

From Ray's Journal:
Another Dreamer..................167

From Ray's Journal:
Moving vs Traveling (Reflections on "Life of Pi")..........170

From Ray's Journal:
The Secret Life of Walter Mitty..................173

From Ray's Journal:
The Way..................176

Suggested for Further Reading..................179

STORYTELLING..................181

The Girl Who Played with Fire by Stieg Larsson..........184

The Girl Who Kicked the Hornet's Nest
by Stieg Larsson..................187

The Girl in the Spider's Web by David Lagercrantz.....191

Alien Hunter by Whitley Strieber..................195

Contents

Deception by John M. Floyd..197

Fifty Mysteries by John M. Floyd................................199

Gates of Fire by Steven Pressfield...........................202

The Haunted Mesa by Louis L'Amour........................204

While the Morning Stars Sing
edited by Lyndon Perry..208

Suggested for Further Reading..................................210

Foreword:
A Book of My Book Reviews

SO why a book of my book reviews? Let me explain.

Like everyone else, I have my themes. There are certain areas of thought and genres of artistic works that I repeatedly go to for knowledge, inspiration, and entertainment. In other words, there are things that appeal to me more than other things. Consequently, if you followed me around, you could likely categorize most of my life's inputs very easily. I'm sure that's true for most people and probably for any aspect of their lives you chose to look at. For me, it's very much reflected in the books I read. When I look at the book reviews I have written, I find they pretty much arrange themselves into categories, because these are the things I like to read about, whether for entertainment or for information.

Now, I began writing and posting reviews of books when I started getting serious about writing and blogging. I considered it a good exercise and a way to get the most from my reading, so over about four years I wrote a lot of reviews. I often referred to them in my blog posts and I included links to them there and on my Facebook, Goodreads, and Booklikes Internet pages. I tended to get my best feedback from these reviews, so when I began considering projects to publish under my Arbordin Park Press imprint (where I had already published my collection of short stories, *The Wider World*), I thought about a compilation of book reviews.

I drew inspiration from Grolier Enterprises' literary annuals of book reviews that they put out from the 1960s through (at least) the 1980s. These annuals were compilations of reviews (100 per annual) of books published in a given year. Each review was an essay, usually 2 to 4 pages in length. While they provided an index of authors, they didn't put the reviews into categories--only alphabetical order.

In this compilation, I've published over 40 book reviews, arranged into categories for which I've also written introductory essays. Within each category, I've included relevant entries from my Internet blog ("Ray's

Ray-views

Journal"), and a short list of books that I think would be helpful for further reading on the category subject.

Since this is a book of my book reviews, I considered entitling it simply, *Ray's Reviews*. Upon reflection, though, it seemed better to shorten that to *Ray-views*.

Each Ray-view starts with some identifying data for the book. These include the author name, ISBN, book type, my rating (5 star scale), and a list of major characters (for fiction). Then I note where the Ray-view was first posted, followed by the Ray-view itself. These are generally a combination of a summary of what the book is about (no spoilers) and an essay on the themes the book contains (or on whatever topics it suggests to me). I selected the blog entries based on their relation to the category subject or on their connection to one or more of the books Ray-viewed in the category. My suggestions for further reading are books I've read, but haven't Ray-viewed, and that I believe will enhance your knowledge of the category subject.

So that's what this is: my thoughts on books I've read that I want to share with you. Each category's essay points out why I think the Ray-viewed books matter to its subject. There are six categories:

Beyond the Usual. That there is more to this life than we generally perceive is an old belief that constantly crops up in drama. Just bear witness to the trend of books concerning vampires, zombies, and now, it seems, angels. Of course, the long-standing genres of Fantasy, Paranormal, Speculative, and their thousand sub-genres attest to the popularity of books (fiction and not) that examine the boundaries of the physical world. Such themes can provide effective plot enhancements for fiction, and be very engrossing subjects for investigation in nonfiction. For this category, I've Ray-viewed both types of books.

The Human Problem. The question of "What's wrong with people?" is at the back of very many dramas, religious writings, and even scientific investigations. It's usually taken for granted that people in general are evil or damaged in some way. That idea is where the "bad guys" come from in drama and it's very much a religious principle for many. But why? Why do humans have this problem when it seems the rest of the Animal Kingdom does not? There are five books that really nailed this for me and I've put them all in this category. The big three of those five are Daniel Quinn's *Ishmael* novels. These seemed just "so right"

Foreword: A Book of My Book Reviews

to me that I began seeing the aspects of Mr. Quinn's arguments in many other books and movies. I think he was building upon Riane Eisler's work, *The Chalice & the Blade*. Then William Golding's classic novel, *Lord of the Flies*, underscores it all with drama. I think these books are very important for a real understanding of humanity's problem, though you won't find a "solution," as such, in them. That requires further research.

On Prophecy. It seems that a lot of people (maybe most people) sometimes get glimpses of the future. They may experience these as Deja-vu or precognitive dreams. These usually concern mundane subjects, but they can also be about significant, and even terrifying, things. The reality of this is examined in an out-of-print book called, *Riddle of the Future*, by Andrew MacKenzie. It's a compelling work that I haven't Ray-viewed, but that I have put in the list of suggested readings for this category. *Riddle* makes the case that, inconceivable as it may be, there is some working of physics that allows for sightings of the future by sensitive persons. If that's the case, then it puts the idea of prophets and seers in a new light that maybe we should pay attention to. John Hogue does just that with a level-headed scholar's knowledge seasoned with a sometimes irreverent humor. He's also a prolific writer with many more books than I've Ray-viewed in this category. These are just the ones I've read. Because I've written so many Ray-views on Mr. Hogue's books, I placed them in a category of their own rather than include them in Beyond the Usual. As a summation of the writings of seers through the ages, and the inspired insights of Mr. Hogue himself, I believe these books have much to offer in considering our current dark times and where humanity is headed.

The Dystopian Potential. Dramatic projections of humanity-on-earth's future tend to be dark. I think it can hardly be otherwise. There are just so many momentums coming together--consequences of the dominator world culture and greed-based human activity as noted in The Human Problem category--that even that majority of people not paying attention have some subconscious feeling that catastrophe is just around the corner. A prelude to that catastrophe is a dystopian world ruled by totalitarian governments (or maybe a single world government). The vision is of an extreme extension of the hierarchal-patriarchal system we live under now. This is a vision that has competed in the past with ones more positive, like *Star Trek* type science fiction futures, but I think the darker view is winning out. I specified "Potential" in the name for this

Ray-views

category because the books I've included in it speak to the possibilities for our future as being one of dystopia. It's a future that stems from class warfare and the books speak to that too--most are fiction, but they are prime examples of fiction-speaking-truth. Their vision is often borne out by the foresight of the seers noted in the books in the On Prophecy category.

Inspiration. People can't live without hope. Losing the belief that life has anything else to offer is the surest killer, as Viktor Frankl discovered in a Nazi death camp. I think this idea is supported by the fact that my journal posts and Ray-views that are inspirational, or that concern works of inspiration, are my most popular. That inspiration can be hard to come by, especially when considering all the evil that runs the world's systems and that is omnicidal in its quest for world dominance. This consideration can easily lead to despair. Many people avoid that despair by adopting the delusion that everything is all right, or that goodness will prevail so not-to-worry. I would rather see things as they are and still find hope, so I latch onto wonderful little books like *The Alchemist* and *Wild*. I let myself be touched by movies like, *The Way*. I look for a strategy to carry on with hope from the pages of *Man's Search for Meaning*, written by a man who knew hopelessness and survived it. And so in the midst of it all, I look for inspiration so that I can inspire.

Storytelling. When it comes to the finer things in life, high on my list is a well-told story. Whatever the medium--book, movie, play, traveling bard--stories inspire and challenge us. They are our examples of how we want to live. They are our metaphors that help us understand the complexities of life. They are what we want to be when we grow up. Stories can be created from sheer imagination or from the God's honest truth. All the Ray-views in this category are for fiction books. While this is a "catch all" category, its focus is on the art of written storytelling, specifically the novel. Whether I've judged the books as good or poor, they all have their lessons and, indeed, they will all be rated with 5 stars on somebody's list. The stories Ray-viewed here are cyber-thriller, mystery, historical fiction, western-fantasy, and speculative. These are genres I love, or am at least curious about, and contain books I recommend (to varying degrees) to entertain, with the potential to inform.

Foreword: A Book of My Book Reviews

OK. So that's what this book is from the standpoint of its construction. By reading it you extract its value, which is my sharing with you the knowledge and enlightenment I have found in the books Ray-viewed. All together, they comprise a base of knowledge that I believe is helpful to understanding current events and humanity's situation. They are the distillations of someone's research and creative soul that have touched me.

I'm pointing you to a feast of which I've partaken, because I know the food is good.

Ray Foy
November 2015

Ray-views

Beyond the Usual

I CALL this category, "Beyond the Usual," because it deals with the extra-dimensionality of life--the idea that life is more than what we see. This idea has been around at least since classical Greece and is a compelling literary device as well as a tenant of belief for many. Of course, it is inherent in the doctrines of the world's major religions, but the purpose of the Ray-views in this category is not to promote books advocating any particular religion. Rather, it is to present a selection of books that considers the trans-dimensional nature of reality.

There is a lot of nonfiction in this list and that probably reflects my tendency to take the study of this subject seriously. But there is fiction here as well because storytelling has always found its firmest foundation on popular spiritual beliefs. Humankind's earliest tales were mythologies describing gods, nonhuman creatures, and experiences that are otherworldly. Even today, the popular stories in books and movies alternate from subjects of vampires to werewolves to zombies to angels, and so on. So there exists among humanity, people that acknowledge the possibility of a greater existence beyond the senses. The books in this category explore such possibilities.

Most people don't really accept the existence of transcendent dimensions until they have an experience with them--they see a ghost, or a UFO, or a living creature considered fanciful. Experiencing the numinous by finding themselves conscious outside of their physical body makes believers out of many people. They might have a Near Death Experience (NDE) where they are declared clinically dead and then revive with memories of their "dead time." They might simply leave their bodies as spirits (or "souls" or "energy," whether intentionally or spontaneously) and have an Out of Body Experience (OBE) where what happens to them is very similar to reports of NDEs. In any case, these are attitude-changing events.

Researcher William Buhlman's book, *Adventures Beyond the Body* is a guidebook to the OBE. It makes a good follow-up to the classic, *Journeys Out of the Body* by the late Robert Monroe. Mr. Buhlman's explorations

Ray-views

verify much of Mr. Monroe's. What we find in both books are descriptions of worlds that exist beyond this physical one. And it seems that if we approach these worlds without dogmas and preconceptions, they present themselves simply as "other places" that we can access and get used to. In fact, both Mr. Buhlman and Mr. Monroe encourage individual exploration of the OBE. Mr. Monroe even founded an institution dedicated to that exploration.

Both books can provide an awakening to the duality of the physical-spiritual nature of the universe and of us. If you read them with an open mind, suspending disbelief, you can begin to build your foundation for accepting the existence of a universe far more expansive than high school physics allows.

With the idea of the physical world extending into the nonphysical (even inhabited) dimensions, it is possible to usefully consider the existence of the numinous reported by those who claim to have traveled there via OBE. A classic work in that area is contained in the volumes written by Carlos Castaneda. He began his researches by studying Yaqui Indian beliefs from an anthropological viewpoint and ended up as the apprentice to a shaman. In a series of books, he recounts his experiences learning from that shaman, Don Juan Matus.

Mr. Castaneda's book, *The Eagle's Gift*, is, I believe, the last in the series and is an interesting picture of a group of people (shaman apprentices) who are fully invested in the transcendent universe. None question the existence of the spiritual realms and are constantly looking for "signs" from them. As I mention in my Ray-view, the book is a strange read, though still compelling for all its strangeness. It is certainly not "scientific" in the way of, say, Mr. Buhlman's book, but it does recognize many characteristics of the transcendent universe as recorded in other, more conventionally grounded works. For that reason, I consider it useful as a "stabilizer" when it comes to entertaining thoughts of nonphysical realms being real and accessible. Spending some time with Mr. Castaneda can give you a reference that may help you better consider other works that expand the boundaries of our usual experience.

One of those other works describes a very direct experience beyond the usual--encountering a Bigfoot (aka, sasquatch). Indeed, *Enoch: A Bigfoot Story* by Autumn Williams describes much more than one man's encounter with a sasquatch. It recounts his ten-year-long interaction with the creature (and its friends). I had never read a book about Bigfoots before this one, though I had read many articles on the subject and seen many TV documentaries. I thought most such books would be

Beyond the Usual

sensationalized, and that seems to be the case, but this one looked different and, in my opinion, it is.

In *Enoch*, Ms Williams presents the very personal story of a witness (she calls him "Mike") who habituated with a group of sasquatches until he was accepted by them (especially the one he calls, "Enoch") as a friend, or at least as nonthreatening. His habituation process was very similar to the one followed by researchers of gorillas and chimpanzees, but the interactions he describes shows these creatures to be of greater intellect than our primate cousins.

In relating Mike's story, Ms Williams does not present sasquatches as supernatural creatures, but she does show them to be more intelligent than any other animal that humans have dealt with in historic times. In fact, their intelligence is more than just a factor of "amount," but is also one of "kind." For instance, there are indications that their communicative skills extend into the telepathic. It seems that a species of very stealthy and intelligent hominids lives among us.

A transcendent view of the universe prompts researches into esoteric areas and it also adds subtle shadings to works of fiction. David Mitchell's work is a prime example of this and so I have included two of his novels in this category. Though Mr. Mitchell indicates that his personal world view is very conventional, the paranormal threads in at least these two novels are very pronounced (and are as well in his latest novel, *Slade House*).

The paranormal theme is especially prominent in *The Bone Clocks* and drives the book's central plot. That plot is a war between "good" and "bad" sets of immortals. The source of their immortality is what puts the immortal individuals on the good or bad side. Their battles include dimension-hopping, time travel, and civilization's fall. It is a science-fiction-paranormal blend that posits a multi-dimensional universe. Mr. Mitchell's theme seems to be that we are more than we appear and simply don't realize our potential. That realization, though, can have bad consequences if we pursue transcendence with immoral motivations. That bad aspect repels the book's main protagonist, Holly Sykes, from paranormal things even when she benefits from them.

Mr. Mitchell's other work in this category, *Cloud Atlas*, is built on a framework of reincarnation. The book is comprised of six novellas, with five presented in two parts. They all encompass some 500 years in time, with a literary connection between each. There is in all of them, the strong implication that the same souls are reappearing as characters in each story's timeframe. As in *Bone Clocks*, this reincarnation thread is a story device, but in the sixth story, Sloosha's Crossin', it is strong with a

Ray-views

paranormal element. It also states the overall theme in *Cloud Atlas* when one character says, "Souls cross ages like clouds cross skies..." This is a really good expression of the transcendence theme found in the works in this category.

I suspect that many people, who accept the transcendent nature of things, believe that the evidence for it can be found in the literary record. *The Historian* by Elizabeth Kostova, advances that view with the tale of a family of scholars who comb the libraries of Eastern Europe searching for the whereabouts of the vampire, Count Dracula (aka, Vlad the Impaler). As Bram Stoker did in his *Dracula* novel, Ms Kostova brings her cast of characters steadily, via research, into knowledge of the supernatural side of the universe and into conflict with one its worst devils (though he turns out to be quite scholarly himself). The takeaway here is the idea of a transcendent universe that can be revealed through open-minded research.

That such research should be performed is the subject of the last Ray-viewed book in this category, *Solving the Communion Enigma* by Whitley Strieber. Mr. Strieber has long been a voice in the UFO/alien abduction community since "coming out" in 1988 to say that he had extensive experiences with such matters. He quickly became a polarizing personality (with people thinking him either a sincere experiencer or a fraud), but over time, he revealed his to be a very reasoned voice. Through his books and his website, he has urged for scientific research to be applied to the UFO phenomena, believing that within it is to be found a rich insight on how we need to live and to cope with these dire times.

I think that one of humanity's great themes is the idea that there is more to life than is presented to the physical senses. It is a persistent theme, especially in art, that people can't let go of. It melds with their religions and is the common baseline of hope for continued existence and finding meaning in life. And so there will always be plenty of books to fill this category.

Adventures Beyond the Body

Author: William Buhlman
Publisher: HarperCollins Publishers
Publication date: 6/28/1996
Pages: 304
ISBN-13: 9780062513717
Type: Nonfiction, Astral Projection, Physics-Philosophy
Ray's rating: 5 stars

The first version of this review appeared on the www.goodreads.com website in June of 2014.

RAY-VIEW

ADVENTURES BEYOND THE BODY is William Buhlman's account of his out-of-body experiences and the inferences he has drawn from them as to the nature of human existence. It is also a guidebook for those seeking to explore the out-of-body experience for themselves.

Mr. Buhlman's book is very much in keeping with the ideas about the nature of the nonphysical dimensions as experienced by Robert Monroe in *Journeys Out of the Body*, and as related by the near death experiencers in Raymond Moody's *Life After Life*. The picture drawn by these is of an "after-life" that is really a continuation of normal, waking life, but at a higher level (or "frequency") in a universe that is multidimensional.

In essence, Mr. Buhlman says our physical world is a low and dense environment that we, as spiritual beings, express ourselves in through physical bodies (flesh-and-blood). We do this, as the consensus among writers on this subject seems to be, in order to grow and develop as sentient beings. The hard knocks of this physical life promotes that growth. As Mr. Buhlman says:

Each of us is currently experiencing the most effective system of growth ever devised: evolution by direct personal experience, by the very act of being.

Mr. Buhlman says that the ability to separate your spiritual (higher energy) self from your physical self (i.e., leave your body) is inherent in everyone and is a very natural and safe thing to do. He even provides instruction on how to do it. That instruction consists of techniques

Ray-views

(relaxation and visualization techniques) that can lead to a conscious separation from the body and an experience of higher frequency environments (sometimes called the spiritual or numinous worlds). He says that daily practice of these techniques usually results in a person being able to attain a successful out-of-body experience (OBE) within thirty days.

Once a person is able to separate from their physical body, Mr. Buhlman suggests they engage in active exploration. In agreement with Robert Monroe, he says the first environment a person will find is the close, energetic one that is a near duplicate of the physical:

> ...*the first nonphysical dimension is a parallel energy world almost identical to the physical universe. This dimension of energy existing close to the physical world is molded by the consensus thoughts of the six billion inhabitants existing in the physical.*

We even have an energy body (often called the "etheric" body) that seems to be especially suited for expression in this near-physical dimension. Mr. Monroe spends more time on it than does Mr. Buhlman, but both recommend separating from this second body in order to explore the higher dimensions ("moving inward" is Mr. Buhlman's term for this further separation and he describes it as a fast, moving or traveling sensation).

Mr. Buhlman also talks a lot about the malleability of the higher frequency environments to sentient thought. That is, when you're there, you think about something (like a park or a house) and it appears. You think about going someplace specific, and you go there (walking or flying--however you imagine). There are even long-lasting environments created by the consensual imaginings of many beings (Heaven and Hell? Vahalla? Disneyworld?). This lends some credence to the premise of *The Secret* and suggests that there is some power to the idea of positive thinking. If our attitudes are building worlds "on the other side," it would be better to build positive ones since we may end up there eventually. This suggests that the Golden Rule is a really good basis for personal morality (because it keeps thoughts positive if actively practiced).

I've read many books on out-of-body experiences (OBE), near-death experiences (NDE), and communications with the dead, so I'm used to such mystical concepts. Readers with a similar background will not freak at *Adventures Beyond the Body* and will, I believe, find it enjoyable and enlightening. I found its biggest value to be its expansion on concepts that Robert Monroe introduced (like techniques for achieving an OBE) and Mr. Buhlman's positive, nonspooky attitude in talking about it all.

Adventures Beyond the Body

For readers new to this subject, I would recommend keeping an open mind and reading without judgment. If you don't dismiss it right off, it will take a while to digest, but you'll be all the better nourished.

The Eagle's Gift

Author: Carlos Castaneda
Publisher: Pocket Books
Publication date: 1982
Pages: 314
ISBN: 0-671-44226-0
Type: Nonfiction, Shamanism, Paranormal, Memoir
Ray's rating: 3 stars
Characters: Carlos Castaneda, Maria Elena (la Gorda), Don Juan Matus, Don Genaro Flores

The first version of this review appeared on the www.goodreads.com website in June of 2014.

RAY-VIEW

THE EAGLE'S GIFT is the last in a series of six books by Carlos Castaneda about the time he spent as an apprentice to a Yaqui Indian shaman called Don Juan Matus. This book focuses (at least in the first part) on Mr. Castaneda's time with the other apprentices of Don Juan, after their master had left them. Even so, the progress of the narrative is not that linear and so Don Juan is a large part of it in flashback. But somewhere around the middle of the book, the narrative seems to meld with the flashback and the thread follows the apprentices' time with Don Juan until his "departure."

This book is not a straightforward read, and there is a "weirdness" about it that will tend to put off readers who are not used to metaphysical works. And this book *is* a metaphysical work. As such, parts of it seem bizarre and nonsensical. That is often the way with this kind of material and it takes some open-minded study to get beyond assertions that challenge the norm of our thinking. If you can do that, you will slowly find, as if in measured revelation, the truths wrapped up in the strange prose.

Mr. Castaneda acknowledges this in the book's prologue. The prose in it is more conventional and is in marked contrast with the writing in the rest of the book. It reveals Mr. Castaneda as an intelligent and literate man, but leads many to consider his books as sheer fiction at best because what he describes is so odd. It is Mr. Castaneda's assertion that his books are true, but that the material "is alien to us; therefore, it seems unreal."

The Eagle's Gift

He began his acquaintance with this material as an anthropologist seeking to study the Mexican Indians' belief system, but he eventually became a practitioner of it.

The Eagle's Gift begins with Mr. Castaneda's return to Mexico when he is seeking out the other apprentices of Don Juan. He had known them from his time there before, though not intimately. When he finds them, his relations with them are tumultuous even though they declare him to be their new teacher and spiritual leader. He does come around to accepting that role, though with the acknowledgement that he still has much to learn.

The apprentices argue and fight (sometimes physically), and go through times of fear and anguish as they constantly look for omens and meanings in the events that happen to them as they seek to follow the path shown to them by Don Juan. Later, they stop working together so much and split into smaller groups. Mr. Castaneda then works exclusively with a woman (Maria Elena whom he calls "la Gorda") who appears to share a special relationship with him, though (in the book at least) it is a spiritual partnership (but it seems to me that a physical relationship is implied). They progress in their work together and achieve a kind of breakthrough when they find they can "dream together," which seems to mean a kind of shared out-of-body experience.

From this point, the narrative includes a lot of Don Juan, but it is unclear as to how much of it is flashback or whether they found Don Juan again. The rest of the book describes the playing out of the mythology, or belief system, of the Indians (called "The Rule of the Nagual") among the apprentices. This section especially takes some study and I expect insight would come from relating it to the other Castaneda books.

I found *The Eagle's Gift* readable, though strange. At times the narrative was compelling and the characters sympathetic, though their actions were sometimes bizarre. But as I said, this is a metaphysical book meant to enlighten more than entertain. I found in it, many concepts that I have also found in other books, though they are expressed in terms of Indian mythology. These include the idea of extra-dimensional universes, humans as extra-dimensional beings, out-of-body experiences beginning as a buzzing or vibration, spiritual awareness achieved through deliberate and practiced concentration (mediation), telepathy, and the constitution of souls as potentially aware and "luminous" after death.

Even so, there are some issues of terminology in this book that are not my preference. For instance, Mr. Castaneda never mentions shamanism but refers to what he and the other apprentices were studying as "sorcery." And among the apprentice sorcerers the designation for the

Ray-views

spiritual seeker is "warrior." Of course, this may be a matter of culture and translation.

I consider *The Eagle's Gift* an important work for the metaphysically minded seeker, and I suspect a study of Mr. Castaneda's works would be enlightening when taken in consideration with that of other metaphysical authors. In that light, I recommend it, though at a lower rating, because it is not as accessible (i.e., "understandable") as it should be.

Enoch: A Bigfoot Story

Author: Autumn Williams
Sold by: Amazon Digital Services, Inc.
Publication Date: 5/18/2015
Print Length: 243 pages
ISBN-13: 978-1-4515499-2-8
Type: Nonfiction, Bigfoot
Ray's rating: 5 stars
Characters: Autumn Williams, "Mike," Enoch (Sasquatch), Cora (Sasquatch), Shelby (Sasquatch)

The first version of this review appeared on the www.goodreads.com, www.booklikes.com, and www.arbordinparkpress.net websites in September of 2015.

RAY-VIEW

I HAVE read a lot of books about things "paranormal" and recognize two common types. One is the "scientific" book that considers all the facts about a phenomena and weighs them logically to reach a conclusion. The other is a recounting of a witness's involvement with the phenomena at a personal level. The second type can be very powerful if it comes off as believable. *Enoch: A Bigfoot Story*, by Autumn Williams, falls solidly into this second type.

Enoch is the story of one man's close involvement with the creature called, "Bigfoot," "sasquatch," or "skunk ape." This involvement took place in the swamps of Florida over ten years and, as far as anyone knows, is still ongoing. The witness is a heavy equipment operator that Ms Williams calls, "Mike." She maintains his personal anonymity and does not reveal the location of his encounters.

I have not read much of the Bigfoot literature but I understand that stories of "long term" witnesses who "habituate" with the creatures are not unknown, though not as widely related as "road crossings" and film clips. This is the first such account I have ever read about and I found it credible and moving.

Ms Williams' interest in Bigfoot began with her own sighting as a child. She was so impressed with the creatures she saw that she began a lifelong study of them (for as much as a thing not recognized by established science can be studied). This eventually led to her being the

Ray-views

host of the cable TV program, *Mysterious Encounters*, which chronicled her leading a team of researchers across the country searching for the creature. The show was much sensationalized. As Ms Williams says:

> *When the series finally began to air, I cringed, finding myself the poster-child for everything that was wrong with Bigfoot research.*

But the series gave her a national platform and, when it was over, it left her with some credentials as a "Bigfoot researcher." From there, she devoted herself to more serious work. That work centered around the website she had established that was built around a database of Bigfoot sightings in Oregon. Her notoriety from cable TV is what prompted "Mike" to contact her about his ongoing relation with a Bigfoot he called, "Enoch." Mike was very reticent about telling his story out of wanting to protect this creature he had come to love as a close friend. Over the course of a year, Ms Williams gained Mike's trust through a series of phone calls and Internet exchanges that finally elicited Mike's story.

That story started at a time when Mike was seeking escape from personal problems in the solitude of the Florida swamp-lands. Like most men of that region, Mike was an avid hunter-fisherman and perfectly at home spending long stretches of time camping in remote areas. During his time of seeking therapy in solitude, he encountered a sasquatch (known locally as a "skunk ape") and deliberately tried to befriend it. He was eventually successful and so began an extended time of interaction.

Mike's description of his habituation with Enoch sounds very much like the process typically gone through with gorillas and chimpanzees. The researcher basically hangs around the group, nonthreateningly, until he or she is accepted. Sharing food is also a big part of the process. Though Enoch was his primary contact, Mike interacted with numerous individuals, especially those that seemed to comprise Enoch's "family."

The picture Mike presents of the sasquatch is that of a very intelligent and social hominid. Like humans, they are omnivores--able to eat most anything, including raw meat. Like early humans, they hunt and gather and even use tools, much as chimpanzees do, though with more refinement. They will use a heavy stick as a club, and even hurl rocks and sticks to kill small game. They vocalize and seem to do so to communicate, though whether actual language is involved was hard for Mike to tell.

I have found that any study of sasquatches usually reaches a paranormal aspect sooner or later. As grounded in gritty reality as Mike's account is, even he seemed to find an extrasensory aspect to the creatures.

Enoch: A Bigfoot Story

He found he could pick up on emotion from them and that they seemed to use that as a means to communicate. For instance, there was a time when he had an altercation with Enoch and later, Enoch expressed his sorrow by reaching out to Mike with waves of sadness. It took a while for Mike to realize what was happening, but when he did, he understood the communication. He says:

> *I was feeling what he was feeling. It was almost like he was trying to let me know that he was afraid - afraid to show himself for fear of what might happen...Right after I got this understanding, I got a strong feeling that he was pleased and happy that I understood.*

The fossil record tells us that at one time, a large number of hominids lived on the earth, human and not. Mike's story indicates that one such race has survived along with us, mostly by being able to eat anything and by staying hidden. Are they as intelligent as humans? That's hard to say from such accounts. Were Neanderthals as intelligent as humans? It seems they were, but they likely expressed their intelligence differently, owing to a different brain structure. The case may be similar for the sasquatch.

Ms Williams came to accept Mike's story based on the strength of his character and on the consistency of his story--both within itself and in comparison with the knowledge of sasquatches she had accumulated over the years. In the process, she describes herself as evolving from a "researcher" to a "witness." This was the big epiphany for her in her understanding of what sasquatches are, and in how to relate to them. This cost her much credibility among Bigfoot "researchers," but then, she came to realize that the usual researchers' methods would only succeed in driving this supremely elusive creature deeper into the woods.

Enoch is a remarkable book. Like Ms Williams, I found the character and self-expressions of Mike to be true to the culture of the society he lives in (that I also grew up in). Also his anecdotes impress me as consistent with what I've read about sasquatches.

I agree with Whitley Strieber that in regards to paranormal (or simply unknown) matters, it is best to maintain an attitude of "keeping the question open." Taking an unbendable stance in such matters, whether to support a scientific or a pet theory, will only tend to prevent discovering the truth. To get the most from Mike's story, Ms Williams recommends that readers go beyond the existential question:

Ray-views

The question, "Does Bigfoot exist?" has been addressed time and time again. Let's move beyond that. For just a moment, let's assume that they do.

If you can do that, you may find the insight that can come from keeping the question open. And it may be an insight that will help you, if you one day find yourself in the deep woods, eye-to-eye with the reciprocal curiosity and fear of a truly untamed creature and distant cousin.

The Bone Clocks

Author: David Mitchell
Publisher: Random House
Publication date: 9/2/2014
Pages: 640
ISBN-13: 978-1400065677
Type: Fiction, Psychological, Thriller, Science Fiction & Fantasy
Ray's rating: 5 stars
Characters: Holly Sykes, Hugo Lamb, Ed Brubeck, Crispin Hershey, Richard Cheeseman, Marinus, Esther Little

The first version of this review appeared on the www.goodreads.com, www.booklikes.com, and www.arbordinparkpress.net websites in March of 2015.

RAY-VIEW

THE BONE CLOCKS is another expansive novel by David Mitchell. At over 600 pages in the hardback edition, it is epic in length and in content. In considering this work with the similar, *Cloud Atlas*, I think Mr. Mitchell may have reinvented the epic saga for our times. Both novels span from 59 to 500 years in their narratives, and even longer in their backstories. They deal with timeless themes, and particularly with the idea of reincarnation, or of souls' survival transcending centuries. In all of it, Mr. Mitchell is examining the threads between lives and expressing the theme of "we're all connected," but also much more.

Where *Cloud Atlas* presented six stories set over 500 years of time, peopled with the same souls in different incarnations, *The Bone Clocks* stays with the span of a single lifetime (59 years), although there are characters in it who have existed for millennia. The novel is also composed of six "novellas," though there is a central story line that connects them. All are told from the point of view of a different character, although the first and last are by the same character (Holly Sykes) at different times in her life. Though they are all connected, each stands on its own, at least from the viewpoint of the narrating character. It is within this framework that Mr. Mitchell works his magic.

The central protagonist, and catalyst, of *The Bone Clocks* is Holly Sykes. We first meet her at the age of 15 when she is running away from home after a major argument with her mother over a boyfriend and a slap

Ray-views

in the face. This is the first "novella" and it follows Holly's experiences and encounters on the road. She has paranormal experiences as she travels, and several of the people she meets play major roles in her life later.

Making incidental or secondary characters from early in the story, major characters later is part of the fun of Mr. Mitchell's books. He's not original in this, but he does it well and it contributes to the tension he maintains throughout. It also underscores the web of relationships that we live in. Even when he's relating the nonheroic events of a person's life, he keeps enough suspense roused to maintain the reader's engagement. You always have the feeling that "this is leading somewhere." And he injects little mysteries (like the periodic appearance of the half-Asian girl with the shaved head) that eventually come to fruition in unexpected ways. For a work of this length, maintaining that reader engagement is a feat of capable storytelling.

In *Cloud Atlas*, Mr. Mitchell displayed a real knack for stylized dialogue, from nineteenth century writing to 1970s era TV crime programs. He doesn't do so much of that in *The Bone Clocks* with the exception of the character of Crispin Hershey, who is a one-hit-wonder author. Hershey's dialogue is a pleasure to read and has a cadence that reminds me of Hugh Grant in all of his films.

There is a strong paranormal vein in *The Bone Clocks*, but it strikes me as not so much an expression of Mr. Mitchell's view of life and the universe, but rather as a plot device. The central storyline that drives all the novellas (whether the narrating characters know it or not) is a war between two competing factions of immortals. One faction is natural immortals that are always reincarnated through a mechanism they don't understand. The other is contrived immortals who attain their reincarnations by basically abducting the bodies of select persons and thus killing their souls. So it's easy to see who the bad guys are.

That main paranormal storyline comes to a head in the fifth novella, "An Horologist's Labyrinth," with a fight between supernaturals that would satisfy any fantasy epic fan, and is the kind of climatic fight scene that should have completed the *Harry Potter* series.

All the novella plots concern Holly Sykes but only the first and last are told by her. The second one is the story of Hugo Lamb as he parties at a Swiss ski resort where Holly is working in a bar. He meets her there and falls in love with her. He also encounters, and is taken in by, the bad faction of immortals.

The third novella is the wedding of Holly and Ed Brubeck (a secondary character from the first novella). Ed is a well-known war

The Bone Clocks

correspondent who has covered all the US Mideast wars at the turn of the 21st century. His main conflict is being torn between his dual loves for family and career.

The fourth novella is about the author, Crispin Hershey, who becomes a good friend of Holly (who gains recognition for herself as a author with a book about her paranormal experiences). Crispin is tortured by an act of revenge he had perpetrated on a reviewer that became a tragedy rather than the simple comeuppance he had intended. The resolution for him involves a confession of cowardice, and maybe some kind of divine judgment.

The fifth novella involves the fight of immortals I mentioned above.

The sixth takes us back to Holly's narration when she is in her seventies. She lives in a world "after the fall" in our near future. Mr. Mitchell's description of this world is, I think, a good extrapolation on where current trends are taking us. It is quite bleak. This part is anticlimactic to the paranormal storyline, but it does play a part.

Mr. Mitchell injects a lot into his stories, almost to the point of being overwhelming, but the levels are presented in an accessible way. The narrative carries readers along easily and leaves them with stores of food for thought that should last for a while. This is Mr. Mitchell's genius and it's what makes me want to read all of his works.

Even so, Mr. Mitchell makes some statements that I don't agree with. In Ed Brubeck's story, he places us in the middle of the Iraq war (i.e., US occupation) from a reporter's eye view. This is interesting material and it should be enlightening to most US readers, as I think it is mostly accurate. He shows the futility of the "war" and gives some feel for the cynical, bombastic, inept arrogance behind it. But I think he doesn't go far enough. He is ultimately too easy on the US. He could have focused on the sheer evil driving that conflict (and associated ones) and tied it to the good vs evil theme of his main storyline. That he didn't (there and at other points) may define lines he can't bring himself to cross.

The Bone Clocks is an engrossing, entertaining, enlightening read that reaches the high bar Mr. Mitchell has set in his other works. It may surpass that bar in that it is more cohesive overall than *Cloud Atlas*. Though I have a few issues with it, it is on my list of all-time favorites and I highly recommend it.

Cloud Atlas

Author: David Mitchell
Publisher: Random House Publishing Group
Publication date: 8/17/2004
Pages: 528
ISBN-13: 9780375507250
Type: Fiction, Fate and Fatalism, Reincarnation
Ray's rating: 5 stars
Characters: Adam Ewing, Autua, Dr. Goose, Robert Frobisher, Rufus Sixsmith, Vyvyan Ayrs, Jocasta Ayrs, Eva van Outryve de Crommelynck, Luisa Rey, Timothy Cavendish, Sonmi-451, Zachry, Meronym, Hae-Joo Chang, Mr. Meeks, Ernie Blacksmith, Nurse Noakes, Javier Gomez, Fay Li, Bill Smoke, Joe Napier, Yoona-939, Isaac Sachs, Old Georgie

The first version of this review appeared on the www.goodreads.com website in August of 2013.

RAY-VIEW

    CLOUD ATLAS is one of the most enjoyable books I've read in a long time. There are a number of aspects that recommend it, but let me tell you, it is a progressive's kind of book. It is an indictment of imperialism, capitalism, and materialism, painted with moral gradients. Mr. Mitchell paints those gradients across a wide canvas, but he does so in a very deliberate, structured way.
    That structure is a telling of six stories--each one being a novella and each with its own definite style and voice taken either from history or invented. The stories span some five hundred years in their settings. The first five are divided at their midpoints with their first halves being told in chronological order until the sixth is reached, told completely, then followed by the second halves of the other five in reverse chronological order. Hence the book's first voice is also its last.
    This divided structure works very well and is even described by one of the characters, a musician, who composes a work by the name of *Cloud Atlas Sextant* which he describes as:

> ...a "*sextet for overlapping soloists*": *piano, clarinet, 'cello, flute, oboe, and violin, each in its own language of key, scale, and color. In the first set, each solo is interrupted*

Cloud Atlas

by its successor: in the second, each interruption is recontinued, in order. Revolutionary or gimmicky?

Well, it works for me. The unique voice of each story is probably the book's most outstanding feature and Mr. Mitchell does an exceptional job with that. I especially liked the voice of the first story, THE PACIFIC JOURNAL OF ADAM EWING. It is set in 1849 and has the sound and "feel" of 19th century writing. The tone, social biases, and even the spelling idiosyncrasies of the time are wonderfully reproduced, making the story sound much akin to the writings of Richard Henry Dana or Charles Darwin. The other stories do the same for the 1930's (the smartass voice of a society leech who is also a musical genius), the 1970's (reads like a screenplay for a TV mystery of that time), 2012 (contemporary, compelling, and even comic), the near future (showing an evolution in language as well as in technology), and the far future ("after the fall", with language being much degraded and most human accomplishment lost).

The other major link among the stories is the idea of reincarnation. Mr. Mitchell plays the idea subtlety and only identifies one soul's reincarnation via the device of a birthmark. The rebirth of others is definitely implied, however, and the movie version does it by having the same group of actors play in each story. The whole of the book is a depiction of reincarnation and Mr. Mitchell even has his characters verbalize that theme at a few points. I think the character, Zachry, says it best:

Souls cross ages like clouds cross skies, an' tho' a cloud's shape nor hue nor size don't stay the same, it's still a cloud an' so is a soul. Who can say where the cloud's blowed from or who the soul'll be 'morrow? Only Sonmi the east an' the west an' the compass an' the atlas, yay, only the atlas o' clouds.

But *Cloud Atlas* is about good-and-evil as much as anything. In a good story, the storytelling is made interesting by the conflicts it describes and that conflict is usually between "good" and "bad" characters. But why is this so? Mr. Mitchell has his two main characters discuss this point in the hinge-pin sixth story, SLOOSHA'S CROSSIN'. His character, Meronym, describes a materialistic view of why there are good and bad people--the good ones can think ahead and put off their needs and so control their own wills, and the bad ones can't. Zachry provides a spiritual counterpoint in that he can see ghosts and demons and so knows there

Ray-views

are dimensions that transcend the physical. Good and bad influences also come from that realm. He says it this way:

Meronym knows a lot 'bout Smart an' life but Valleysmen know more 'bout death.

By the time you reach the last section of the book, which is the conclusion of the first novella, Mr. Mitchell has covered a lot of ground and seems to want to leave the reader with some sense of what it's all about ("life" that is). He reiterates the material view of evil in the world with one character's personal law of survival: "The weak are meat the strong do eat." Then he gives the last word to the voice he started with, Adam Ewing, which also seems to be a call to activism. After his far travels and adventures, Mr. Ewing decides how he'll spend the remainder of his years (note: Jackson is his son):

A life spent shaping a world I want Jackson to inherit, not one I fear Jackson shall inherit, this strikes me as a life worth the living.

In this statement, put down in his journal, Ewing has a moment of prescience along with his insight (the "advanced" tribe in SLOOSHA'S CROSSIN' is called the "Prescients"). It's like he, a character in the book, is stepping outside the book to comment on its sweeping epic. This complements the reincarnation theme and the forward-in-time/backward-in-time literary structure that amounts to a defiance of the linearity of time. Like Ewing, it leads us to step outside of time and consider what's important. What shall we do?

And so *Cloud Atlas* goes high on my list of all-time favorite books. It is ingenious in structure, thoughtful in tone, compelling in story, delightful in prose, and progressive in theme. It provides thoughtful readers with much to ponder in considering this time in which they are living, and maybe even for those times they have already lived, and will live.

The Historian

Author: Elizabeth Kostova
Publisher: Little, Brown and Company
Publication date: 6/1/2005
Pages: 704
ASIN: B000FCK6EI
Type: Science Fiction and Fantasy, Vampires, Myths and Legends
Ray's rating: 4 stars
Characters: Paul and his daughter, Helen Rossi, Bartholomew Rossi, Vlad Dracula

The first version of this review appeared on the www.goodreads.com, www.booklikes.com, and www.arbordinparkpress.net websites in July of 2015.

RAY-VIEW

THE HISTORIAN is Elizabeth Kostova's long novel about a group of people's search to find and destroy the vampire, Dracula. Yes, this is the same Dracula who is the object of Bram Stoker's classic novel and inspired by the historic ruler of Wallachia (next door to Transylvania), resister of the Ottoman Empire, also known as "Vlad the Impaler." In fact, Stoker's novel is part of this novel's universe and is mentioned several times. In the course of Ms Kostova's book, readers learn a good bit about the historical Dracula, as well as about life in the Romanian part of eastern Europe. The vehicle for the search for Dracula, scholarly research, is (for the most part) compellingly described. Moments of horror punctuate the narrative and lead to a satisfying portrayal of the Impaler himself.

Ms Kostova's admiration of Bram Stoker's book is seen in her numerous mentions of it. She even borrowed a story feature from it, where a group of human allies are bonding in their quest to find and destroy a great evil. Some of them even bond romantically, just as in Stoker's novel, contributing to the family relationship of the vampire hunters. Another device she borrows from Stoker is the narrative consisting of documents written by the characters. These are made up of letters and journals and some are even noted as being inserted by a given character for the sake of providing completeness to the tale. This makes the narrative personal accounts rotating among several of the main characters, just as in Stoker's book. It is not done in a distracting way and the general feel is simply of a story told in first-person. And that story is in a modern format, with contemporary sensibilities, and without the "tritely romantic" or patriarchic aspects of Stoker's book.

But the overriding theme and tone of *The Historian* is the sheer love of books and scholarship, especially historical scholarship, by the characters. The search for Dracula is mostly carried out in libraries--public libraries and the private libraries of monasteries and of the scholar-vampire hunters. This could make for a dry narrative but it does not in *The Historian*, which I attribute to the storytelling ability of the author and her obvious passion for literary study and research. Readers of like mind will appreciate this aspect.

Ms Kostova pairs that love of scholarship with a love of travel. The characters travel a lot throughout Europe and we see in them the appreciation of exotic locales, cafes, foods, coffees, and wines. This melding of literary appreciation, scholarship, and traveling is what makes *The Historian* most memorable for me, and it is done--for the most part-- without sacrificing the storytelling or slowing the plot.

I say, "for the most part," because I think Ms Kostova does carry the travels, library searches, misdirections and dead-ends a bit too far before she reaches her finale. I think she could have cut a lot of that and reduced the length of her book by about one third without any loss to the story. It would have made the book's good parts even stronger. That burdensome excess cost the book a star in my rating.

Still, the good parts show that love of learning that is so second-nature to the characters and it comes out in some neat ways. Like when a mother meets her daughter after a long separation and offers her a high complement:

She looked at me for a moment, her head to one side. "You are a historian," she said after a moment. It wasn't a question.

In a romantic scene when Paul is observing his love interest, his desire is stimulated by the inclusion of a book in her hands:

...I liked the way she lay sprawled across our hotel bed in Perpignan, flipping through a history of French architecture that I'd bought in Paris.

French architecture! And he had already read the book! But the characters are not just total book-nerds. They take action when they need to: wielding guns, knives, stakes, and garlic against the undead. And at

The Historian

times, they look up and notice beauty in the physical world, especially when it's an embodiment of descriptions from ancient manuscripts. For example, Paul and Helen are blown away when they visit the Hagia Sophia in Istanbul for the first time. The sheer beauty of its architecture inspires a desire in Paul to live more fully in the wider world, outside of books:

Looking back at that moment, I understood that I had lived in books so long...that I had become compressed by them internally. Suddenly, in this echoing house of Byzantium--one of the wonders of history--my spirit leaped out of its confines. I knew in that instant that, whatever happened, I could never go back to my old constraints. I wanted to follow life upward...

So we follow these library-loving scholars in their search for Dracula through three-fourths of the book before we finally encounter the five hundred year-old vampire. By that time, we've learned enough of the historic Vlad to get a feel for the kind of person he was, and then the presentation of him as a character complements that knowledge. He is presented with all the arrogance and psychopathy of the ruler-impaler, and yet he is also another scholar:

Perhaps you do not know that I was something of a scholar. This seems not widely known...I became an historian in order to preserve my own history forever...I am a scholar at heart, as well as a warrior, and these books have kept me company through my long years.

Even Dracula's relating of how he became a vampire through his search for the means of achieving immortality, included the vehicle of a book:

But recently I met a man, a merchant who has traveled to a monastery in the West. He said there is a place in Gaul, the oldest church in their part of the world, where some of the Latin monks have outwitted death by secret means. He offered to sell me their secrets, which he has inscribed in a book.

Appropriate. *The Historian* is a really neat work of fiction that is on my list of favorites because of its unapologetic love of books and learning, coupled with a stimulating vision of one of history's monsters brought to undead life. If you are a lover of books and appreciate the intellectual excitement of searching for the resolution of mysteries in the historical record, then you'll find hanging on through *The Historian*'s 700+ pages a rewarding experience.

Solving the Communion Enigma

Author: Whitley Strieber
Publisher: Penguin Group (USA)
Publication date: 2011
Pages: 216
ISBN-13: 978-1-585-42917-2
Type: Nonfiction, Metaphysics
My rating: 4 stars

The first version of this review appeared on the www.goodreads.com website in June of 2012.

RAY-VIEW

WHEN Whitley Strieber's book, *Communion*, came out in 1988, it was the first major work on the UFO phenomenon to be published in a while. Mr. Strieber was already known as a horror writer and had had some success with his novels, *Warday*, *Wolfen*, and *The Hunger*. So the question surrounding his latest book at that time was: Is he telling the truth, or just trying to make money?

Having followed Mr. Strieber's career and writings since *Communion*, I believe the former. He is being as honest as it's possible to be in telling a difficult and strange story.

Solving the Communion Enigma is Mr. Strieber's summation of the journey that began for him with the *Communion* experience, which was an apparent abduction by alien entities on December 26, 1985. While his relating of that event led to his being identified with the popular notions of "alien abduction," he has never been an adherent to that interpretation for what happened to him. He does not dismiss the possibility completely because he finds value in keeping the question open, but he does not aver that his visitors were from another planet. In *Solving the Communion Enigma* he says:

> *Being identified as a believer in aliens has always troubled me. It just doesn't seem to me to be the only possible explanation.*

Another famous UFO researcher, Jacques Vallee, came to a similar conclusion in his book, *Dimensions*. After relating some of the more exotic of UFO anecdotes, he describes the logical expectations of alien

Solving the Communion Enigma

visitations and concludes that "aliens from another planet" just isn't a strange enough explanation for the UFO phenomenon.

So what is? That's the question Mr. Strieber has been trying to answer, or at least address, in the years since his *Communion* incident.

Solving the Communion Enigma is a record of Mr. Strieber's years of engagement with the phenomena. Followers of his writings, in both his nonfiction books and on his website, will recognize much of the material and be enlightened from his further observations. They begin right after the *Communion* incident, when Mr. Strieber sought to engage the beings that assaulted him that fateful night. Or maybe I should say he *continued* to engage them, since he later came to believe the contacts started in his childhood but were suppressed. He describes this in Part One and advances the theory that childhood traumas, whether by chance or manipulated, can open a person to this contact.

It can also open a person to invasive trauma, like having objects implanted in their bodies. I was aware that Mr. Strieber had claimed to be the recipient of such an implant and had even tried to have it removed, but I had not read about it in detail. He describes what implants are and relates his own experience in Part One. It is fascinating material and I can see why the study of such implants would be a way to bring a scientific angle to the abduction phenomena, if any credentialed scientists would do it.

I had also not read at length about crop circles and he has a section in Part Two about that. Like implants, there's more to the subject than I realized and it seems to be another topic worthy of real scientific study.

In Part Three, Mr. Strieber gets more into his personal experiences with beings that might be alien, or humans from a different plane or state of development. His experiences are in keeping with much mystic lore, both modern and classical. His descriptions of his times of meditating with these beings, the symbolic insights they offered, and the richness of his time with them are fascinating. His premiere experience of this kind was with the "Master of the Key," an apparently human male whom he met in Canada and conversed with in the early morning hours. He related the insights he gained from their conversation in his book, *The Key*.

Mr. Strieber relates all this other-worldly material in tight, engaging prose. Reading his work is like listening to an intelligent dinner guest talk about exotic, engrossing, subjects, who is also not afraid to let some emotion come through. In fact, he relates some really personal things, but that is also typical of his writings and a testament to his honesty.

Early in *Solving the Communion Enigma* Mr. Strieber says "Something about this world of ours simply does not add up." Many agree, though

Ray-views

what it is in particular is a matter of considerable argument. Pet doctrines that adherents can't bear to see contradicted fill the gaps in our knowledge and offer the solace of ignorance to true believers. But UFOs and the phenomena that surround them are notorious for contradicting reality (as we know it), and laying waste to theories that seek to explain them. They deny themselves just as human authorities deny them, and while other factions embrace them as real space aliens. Experiencers, like Mr. Strieber, are caught in the middle and are alternately lauded and hated.

Yet it is this very tension that may be the whole purpose of the UFO/alien abduction experience. Trying to understand the contradictions and the positive and negative passions they arouse may be the force exerted by the intelligence behind the UFOs to actually change the way humans think. As Mr. Strieber says, it may be the very force of evolution as applied to humanity.

If so, then finding a productive way to engage the UFO phenomena is one of humanity's greatest quests, and Mr. Strieber is a pioneer in trying to show us the way. *Solving the Communion Enigma* is a very helpful tool towards reaching that engagement.

There is Something Here Among Us

Source: Ray's Journal, www.rayfoy.com, 15-Jul-2012

I REMEMBER when Whitley Strieber's book, *Communion*, came out in 1988. It had been a while since any major UFO books had been published, and there was some media attention that caught my eye. Having an old interest in the UFO subject, I looked for the book and found it in a mall book store. The clerk who took my money noted what I was buying and asked me the question that was in general circulation at the time:

"You think he's telling the truth, or just trying to make money?"

I didn't have a good answer. I said something like, "I don't know, I'll see what he has to say." After all these years, I'd say he wasn't out to just make money. He would have made more if he had never said anything about UFOs or aliens, but those topics came to define his life.

I don't "believe in aliens" any more than Mr. Strieber does. The Star Trek idea of high-tech aliens exploring the galaxy falls apart from a realization of the sheer enormity of the universe. As Mr. Strieber notes in *Solving the Communion Enigma*, even light-speed is slow when trying to get around the Milky Way. And as Jacques Vallee says, the "aliens from another planet" hypothesis is just not strange enough to explain the UFO phenomena as it is reported by experiencers.

So what's happening? What are UFOs and alien abductions?

Having spent many years reading about that and related phenomena, having some experiences myself, and hearing others talk of their experiences, I believe it is real. But what it is, has to do with our perception of reality and that includes our perceptions about death. Many UFO anecdotes include dead people as well as "aliens." In fact, there are strong similarities between UFO stories and Near Death Experiences. Kenneth Ring explored those connections in his book, *The Omega Project*.

When I was a child in the 1960s, the United States was undergoing a major "UFO flap," that is, there were a lot of sightings being reported. While there was skepticism, there was not the stigma and high ridicule showered on experiencers that there is now. UFO sightings were reported

Ray-views

in the newspapers and magazines, and they were discussed on television. Today, if they are not mentioned in the context of sheer fiction, they are dismissed with contempt. Back then, however, they grabbed my interest and hold it to this day. In the 1980s, Whitley Strieber was one of the few voices that spoke seriously of the UFO phenomena and so I followed what he had to say, even when he was ridiculed.

It's not easy to read Mr. Strieber's books, and I've read them for many years now. He challenges our perceptions of reality and dares us to truly think "outside the box." That can be difficult and even frightening. In *Solving the Communion Enigma*, Mr. Strieber says:

There is something here among us that acts in an intelligent manner, but not in ways that we might act.

I believe seeing that "something," let alone engaging with it, is a matter of perception. Perceiving in such a manner requires letting go of cherished delusions and daring to see things as they are, and realizing that even if we were to see reality without filters, we might not understand it or even want it.

That's the price of seeking reality.

My Issues with The Bone Clocks

Source: Ray's Journal, www.rayfoy.com, 10-Apr-2015

I AM a big fan of David Mitchell, author of *Cloud Atlas*. I love his prose and the way he weaves a story together from a very intricate web of characters and events, often spanning a timeframe of centuries. His plotting keeps the reader engrossed, whether depicting a battle of immortals or an author plotting revenge on a critical reviewer. All these elements are at work in Mr. Mitchell's latest novel, *The Bone Clocks*, that I recently read and Ray-viewed. I loved the book, but even so, Mr. Mitchell made a few points in it that I disagree with.

Now I noted in my Ray-view that the book has a section set in the Iraq "war" that is one character's recollections. I thought it was well done and really put the reader on the ground, from a journalist's viewpoint, amidst all the senseless violence. I thought it didn't go far enough, however, in denouncing the criminality of that conflict, and so I was a bit uncomfortable with it. Still, I can forgive that. What really prompts me to comment, are a couple of other passages in the book.

The first is from one character's internal monologue:

...I take a deep, shuddery breath to stop myself crying...it's everything: It's grief for the regions we deadlanded, the ice caps we melted, the Gulf Stream we redirected, the rivers we drained, the coasts we flooded, the lakes we choked with crap, the seas we killed, the species we drove to extinction, the pollinators we wiped out, the oil we squandered, the drugs we rendered impotent, the comforting liars we voted into office--all so we didn't have to change our cozy lifestyles...we summoned it, with every tank of oil we burned our way through. My generation were diners stuffing ourselves senseless at the Restaurant of the Earth's Riches knowing--while denying--that we'd be doing a runner and leaving our grandchildren a tab that can never be paid. (David Mitchell, *The Bone Clocks*, Random House, 2014 edition, p560-561)

I agree with his assessment here of the current state of the world. I don't completely agree, though, that things are this way because we are selfish louts consuming the world's resources without thought, and that

Ray-views

we do so at the expense of the next generations. Yes, people do that, but they are driven by a "dominator" culture that is parasitic to humanity and run by a psychopathic, patriarchal, oligarchy. It is these, at the top of the pyramid, that are ultimately responsible for our planet's destruction and I will not take the blame for them. I did not vote liars into office. The system will only put liars into office, regardless of whom I vote for (if I really had a vote).

So does that mean that you and I have no responsibility for the state of the world? Certainly not. I believe it behooves us to do what is right and to resist evil as much as we can. It's just that I will not, in doing so, pretend that the world's ills are a result of common thoughtlessness (basically, gluttony). No, there is a driving evil for this that we, the common people, have not been able to overthrow in ten thousand years.

It is best not to engage in mindless consumption as if the earth were a limitless resource, and so believe that tomorrow will always be like today. That is delusion and is a support of the oligarchs. In fact, they depend upon our maintaining that delusion. We can fight them, and erode their system only to the extent that we can awaken to reality.

Now considering the above, there is another passage in *The Bone Clocks* that I found most interesting and probably indicative of Mr. Mitchell's mindset:

Unthinkingly, I've looked up at the sky. My imagination can still project a tiny glinting plane onto the blue...a jet airliner, its vapor trail going from sharp white line to straggly cotton wool. (David Mitchell, *The Bone Clocks*, Random House, 2014 edition, p565)

This is a description of a small part of what we see over our heads every day--high flying airplanes leaving long aerosol trails that don't dissipate, but expand like (ugly) "straggly cotton wool." This is Stratospheric Aerosol Geoengineering (SAG) that is currently the principal means for the oligarchs' destruction of the earth. In averring that this describes a "vapor trail," perhaps Mr. Mitchell has reached another line that he cannot cross.

As an author, David Mitchell is currently enjoying a popularity and influence that rivals J. K. Rowling at the height of her *Harry Potter* series. So it is fascinating to see that he even touches on issues that lead to a consideration of the world as it really is. Most fiction writers do not. They stay within the accepted constraints of their genre.

Perhaps if we can cross that line ourselves, in our thinking and in our actions, we can encourage our artists and bards to do the same. It is

My Issues with The Bone Clocks

only there, beyond the line, that we have any chance of finding a better world.

Suggested for Further Reading

Journeys Out of the Body by Robert Monroe

Crossing Over by John Edward

Lessons from the Light by George Anderson

At Peace in the Light by Dannion Brinkley

Slade House by David Mitchell

www.geoengineeringwatch.org

The Human Problem

THE BOOKS in this category address the basic problem that besets humanity: why is the human race so bad? Why can't humans live at peace with nature and each other when all other animals can (that kill only for food and live sustainably)? In *The Chalice & the Blade*, Riane Eisler states the question better than anywhere else I've seen it:

What is it that chronically tilts us towards cruelty rather than kindness, towards war rather than peace, toward destruction rather than actualization?

The question is especially relevant for this current time when the very survival of all life on earth is in question, and only the most deluded can doubt that human agency is not the cause. And that agency looks to be very deliberate in its working.

This problem has been long known in human history, though it is usually addressed through religion. In the books Ray-viewed for this category, the problem is addressed through anthropology, history, and mythology. What the authors have found is that there was a time of definite, deliberate change in the organization of human affairs. One way of living was replaced by another. And though it did not happen overnight, the change was relentless in wiping out the old ways. It reached a critical mass millennia ago, but continues to this day, and it will continue (by its own mandate) until every last trace of any other mode of living is obliterated.

Three of the books in this category were written by Daniel Quinn, who created a very descriptive terminology for the ways-of-life, or cultures, that we're talking about. He avers that the dominant human mode of living before the great change was hunter-gather. That society was cooperative and partnering rather than competitive and hierarchical. Men and women were, as Ms Eisler says, partners and their dominant deities were goddesses because they saw human life as beginning with the female. Mr. Quinn calls them "Leavers" because their defining trait was that they *left* decisions of who lives and who dies in the hands of the gods.

Ray-views

Mr. Quinn goes on to say that the Leavers were rivaled by, and eventually replaced by, the Takers. These were people who decided it was better to quit hunting and gathering, stay in one place to grow crops, raise livestock, and build cities. This was that period in human history known to anthropologists as "the agricultural revolution." Overall, it was an inferior way to live for the most of humanity but the establishment of skills specialization and hierarchy made it stick (aided by "locking up the food," as Ishmael says). It was a system very rewarding to those few who fought their way to the top of the hierarchy and who, once there, would not leave it. Such was the power they commanded that they were able to *take* from the gods the decisions of who lives and who dies.

This is not to say that the Leavers did not, or would not, settle to grow crops and build settlements. The evidence is that they did (like in Crete). The difference is that in doing so, they remained Leavers, promoting cooperation over competition, and partnership over patriarchy.

The Chalice & the Blade takes this line of thought to more definite levels, showing that the society of Crete left much evidence of goddess worship and cooperative living. It identifies the main source population group for the Takers as being the Kurgan people from the Caucasus region north of Turkey (hence, Mr. Quinn speculates, the "Mark of Cain" might have been white skin).

These four nonfiction books are very powerful to me, making better sense of human society and cultures than anything else I've ever read. They make understandable the Biblical stories of Adam and Eve, and of Cain and Abel. In a nutshell, the story of the first humans being cast from the perfect garden due to evil is a beautiful picture of the hunter-gather life being taken from people by a power that is motivated by vaunting, Satan-like pride and a desire to "play God."

This "fall" is also shown in the Cain and Abel story, where Cain, the herdsman, is killed by Abel, the farmer and city dweller. They are brothers, but the one feels privileged to decide his brother's fate. It is the Takers killing the Leavers. It is the Kurgans killing the Cretans.

One area that, curiously, neither Mr. Quinn nor Ms Eisler go into, is the "why" of the change. Why did this group of Takers make the move to settled agriculture supported by hierarchy and then fight to hang onto it. I believe that question is answered in the last book Ray-viewed in this category, *Lord of the Flies.*

William Golding's book is the only fiction in this category, but it is a prime example of fiction telling truth. This classic work about preadolescent boys falling into "savagery" when they are stranded on a

The Human Problem

deserted island without adults, shows us why there are factions that push the Taker-Dominator organization onto things.

Among the boys on the island, there is bravery, heroism, even intelligence and a love of beauty. But those things cannot withstand the determined pursuit of power by Jack, the psychopath. He has little regard for human life and even becomes fascinated with the idea of killing. He wants to rule the island, decide who lives and who dies, and in this he is relentless. We live in a society that selects for the Jacks, and pushes them to the top of its organizing structures.

Because destruction is at the very core nature of the Taker culture, its end can only be the destruction of itself and of as much of other life-on-earth that it can reach. Certainly, this is insane and in keeping with the psychopathic mindset that fuels it. In *Bury My Heart at Wounded Knee*, Dee Brown describes the mystification of the American indigenous peoples (Leavers) with the destructive character of the white people who are displacing them. That obsession with death and destroying defines US foreign policy and the governments of the world (especially the Western world) to this day.

I believe that understanding the books in this category is vitally important for understanding the way the world really is. The solution they imply is the replacing of the Taker (or "dominator") culture with the cooperative, Leaver culture (Neo-Tribal). This can be done without reverting to a Neolithic level of living (though that may happen for other reasons). How likely is that? Not very, considering the power for destruction on a global scale that electronic technology has given our rulers. The only question is whether the world will be lucky enough to survive the Takers. It seems that that outcome can only be left in the hands of the gods.

Ishmael: An Adventure of the Mind and Spirit

Author: Daniel Quinn
Publisher: Random House Publishing Group
Publication date: 5/28/1995
Pages: 272
ISBN-13: 9780553375404
Type: Fiction, Religious and Inspirational, Science Fiction and Fantasy, Anthropology
Ray's rating: 5 stars
Characters: Ishmael, Alan Lomax (not named)

The first version of this review appeared on the www.goodreads.com website in May of 2012.

RAY-VIEW

RIGID social hierarchy, constant competition, commodifi'cation of all things, destructive exploitation of the natural environment, endless war for profit, comfort for a few and mind-numbing toil for most. These are the features of modern life that are accepted by the majority of people (especially Americans) and exploited with gusto by the uppermost tier of the extremely wealthy.

Why is human society like this?

That's the question addressed by Daniel Quinn's "teaching" novel, *Ishmael: An Adventure of the Mind and Spirit*. He addresses it through a Socratic dialogue between an old, intelligent, lowland gorilla named, Ishmael, and his student--a burnt-out writer who left his optimism behind in the sixties. Obviously, this is a speculative fiction, but that fiction carries Quinn's thesis describing why things are the way they are, and it does so in an utterly engaging way. In the midst of all the anthropological history and questions-and-answers, Quinn never forgets that he's telling a story. Ishmael and his unnamed student gain our admiration and sympathy. Though there's not a lot of physical action, there is drama, and we care about what happens to these characters.

Even though Quinn gives us sympathetic characters to relate to, it is the intellectual journey the reader takes through Ishmael's teachings that give the book its power and have made it a "cult classic." That journey is a relating of human history from the standpoint of the great divide that took place around 8000 BC. What divided was a group of humans that

Ishmael

Ishmael calls the "Takers" from the rest of humanity he calls the "Leavers." The Takers cultivated land, domesticated animals, established cities, created writing, and, in a nutshell, launched Western civilization. As they did so, they displaced, absorbed, and killed, the hunting-gathering groups of Leavers around them. This time is usually associated with the founding of the world's earliest cities, supported by agriculture, by the Sumerians in the Middle East (in the Tigris-Euphrates valley, also known as "Eden"). James Burke, in his television documentary series of the Seventies called *Connections*, depicted this time as beginning with the invention of the plow. Ishmael would probably consider that an appropriate symbol for the Takers.

But this book is not just a history lesson. Mr. Quinn's genius lies in his distillation of Neolithic events to explain why, after three million years of successfully living as a part of nature, humans decided to make their way by conquering it, subduing it, and growing "without limit" at its expense. He applies the story of Cain and Abel to this turning point in a way that makes more sense of that myth than any I have ever heard. Quinn also explains why this pivotal turn in human affairs is ultimately fatal.

Ishmael is an important book. I believe it is very helpful to anyone seeking to make sense of this dire time we live in and that Mr. Quinn's overall thesis is right-on. I would disagree with him, though, on a few points. For instance, I think Ishmael's timeline for the Leavers is too long, at least for homo sapiens. Three million years past would include prehumans like homo erectus and homo habilis. I'm not sure that including them supports his point of Takers not being an evolution of Leavers. I also disagree that the fall of the Soviet Union was anything to be optimistic about with regard to hope for humanity's future. I see it as just an event in the constant warfare among groups of Takers.

Still, if you're looking for answers, if you're a seeker for truth, I highly, highly recommend *Ishmael*. Someone looking only for a story will probably be put off by the format (Socratic dialogue) and the lack of a dominant plot, but the seeker should note the subtitle: *An Adventure of the Mind and Spirit*. It is just that. The story's plot is the one we're all living, whether we're aware of it or not. I think most of us are not aware, and awareness is vital.

One interesting aspect of this story is how Mr. Quinn describes Ishmael's growing intelligence as a function of his increasing awareness since he was taken from Africa. This book will increase your awareness of life the way it really is, if you let it. And if you let it, it will give you

Ray-views

some keen insight into why things are the way they are, and provide a foundation to build on.

After reading *Ishmael*, I reread Jared Diamond's *Guns, Germs, and Steel* and found that the two texts greatly enlightened each other. It's the kind of study and comparison that Ishmael would encourage. He believed that the answers are there in the literature, for anyone who will look.

I'm looking. I feel compelled to. If you feel the same, you'll love *Ishmael*.

The Story of B

Author: Daniel Quinn
Publisher: Random House Publishing Group
Publication date: 11/28/1997
Pages: 352
ISBN-13: 9780553379013
Type: Fiction, Religious and Inspirational, Science Fiction & Fantasy, Anthropology
Ray's rating: 4 stars
Characters: Jared Osborne, Charles Atterley, Shirin, Father Lulfre

The first version of this review appeared on the www.goodreads.com website in May of 2014.

RAY-VIEW

    THE STORY OF B is the second book in Daniel Quinn's *Ishmael* trilogy. These books are a trilogy not so much in that they are the continuation of a story, but in that they are a continuation of a single teaching that each elucidates with its own slant. The only common fictional element is the character, Ishmael, though he is hardly more than referenced in *The Story of B*. That reference, however, lends its verification to Mr. Quinn's core teaching and lets you know that this book has its place among the three (*Ishmael, The Story of B, My Ishmael*--I suggest you read the books in that order). That teaching is the value of these books.
    And that teaching is the (in my opinion) brilliant, startling, enlightening, and intellectually (and even spiritually) satisfying proposition that the problems of our current civilization stem from a single human culture that has spread and dominated the world since the Agricultural Revolution occurred some 10,000 years ago. Mr. Quinn refers to that revolutionary agriculture as "totalitarian agriculture" in *The Story of B*. It is based on the hallmark premise of the culture that created it, that their way is the only "right" way to live and that all opposition must be utterly destroyed. The rise of this culture (called "The Takers" by Mr. Quinn) is mythically described in the Genesis stories of Adam and Eve's Fall and in the Slaying of Abel by Cain.
    Mr. Quinn says the problem with this Taker culture, especially in our time, is that it...

Ray-views

...isn't working--doesn't work and can't work. It bears with it its own seeds of destruction. It's fundamentally unstable.

Mr. Quinn expresses this teaching through fiction in all three books, and most engagingly in the Ishmael books. In all of them, the point of view is that of a student seeking the knowledge offered by a sage who wants to oppose the evils of the Taker culture by changing the minds of his students. This fictional premise works well largely due to the interesting and compelling character of Ishmael who is an intelligent, self-aware, gorilla. In *The Story of B*, the teacher is actually the head of a group of "coffee house intellectuals" and is simply referred to as "B." The implication is that this head teacher changes over time. The one that the student-protagonist in *The Story of B* deals with is Charles Atterly.

That "student" is Jared Osborne, a Roman Catholic priest. He is sent by his superior, Father Lulfre, to Germany to investigate the teachings of Atterly that have had enough impact so as to come to the attention of the Church. Lulfre also wants Osborne to gather information to help determine whether Atterly might be the Antichrist, because finding the Antichrist is a prime mission of Lulfre's order, the Laurentians. So one story in *The Story of B* is Osborne's working of this mission. In the course of it, he becomes caught up in B's teachings (they are another story of B) and duly records them. I expect you can guess the rest.

Mr. Quinn is a good writer and *The Story of B* held my interest. I liked the idea of the coffee house group and of its changing leadership. Some insights are offered about the thinking and humanness of a Catholic priest that make Osborne a sympathetic character, but even so, I have some criticisms.

Osborne starts out as a well educated and committed priest. Indeed, of the three books, he is (or should be) the most intellectually capable of all the students presented. As such, he should have had more to offer in his discourses with B, especially more initial opposition. And that opposition should have been based more on his priesthood training. There are moments when he does this, but they are brief and cut off too soon. Consequently, he comes off as being *too* accepting of B's teachings and *too* readily a convert. In contrast, the students in the Ishmael books come upon their teacher's insights in a more believable fashion, making it easier for the reader to share in their intellectual discovery.

Also, while I am not familiar with the Catholic order of the Laurentians, I wonder if they are as ruthless as presented by Mr. Quinn. They come off as a bit mafia-like. While that's obviously for the sake of

The Story of B

drama, it's a bit of a stretch. It might also come from Mr. Quinn's apparent disdain for the spiritual, or anything he considers "nonscientific."

The Story of B is an expansion and clarification on the teaching offered in *Ishmael*. It's not a big expansion--it doesn't break much new ground--but it does offer the basic premise in a way that may be more straightforward than it was in *Ishmael*. Mr. Quinn does this in the very structure of the book. The first part is the telling of the story of Jared Osborne and his search for, and engagement with, B. In this part, he doesn't give the actual words of B in his lectures, but just Osborne's reaction to them. Enough is given to provide the reader with the basic idea's of B's teachings, but the actual lectures are saved for an afterword labeled, "The Public Teachings." This works and facilitates the book's use as a reference.

The Story of B is part of a trilogy of Mr. Quinn's books that I consider essential reading for anyone seeking to understand why the world is the way it is. For the open-minded, critical reader, these books have a tremendous insight to offer. That's why so many reviews refer to them as "life changing." While *The Story of B* has some dramatic shortcomings, it is still enjoyable, enlightening, and one of my favorite books.

My Ishmael: A Sequel

Author: Daniel Quinn
Publisher: Random House Publishing Group
Publication date: 10/6/1998
Pages: 304
ISBN-13: 9780553379655
Type: Fiction, Religious and Inspirational, Science Fiction & Fantasy, Anthropology
Ray's rating: 4 stars
Characters: Ishmael, Julie Gerchak, Alan Lomax, Art Owens

The first version of this review appeared on the www.goodreads.com website in March of 2013.

RAY-VIEW

I THINK Daniel Quinn has hit upon something very special in his *Ishmael* books. That special thing is a concept, or way of looking at human history, that tells the story of how people came to be the way they are. Mr. Quinn tells this story through his fictional teacher who seeks students to learn his insights and pass them on. That teacher is a sentient gorilla by the name of Ishmael.

Ishmael teaches by telling stories and engaging his pupils in a Socratic dialogue. He wants to lead them through a string of linked concepts and so get them to figure his lessons out for themselves. This can be trying for his students, but is so much more effective than if he had, say, tossed them something printed to memorize. His students become quite passionate about what they learn and so vindicate his methods.

Of course, it is Mr. Quinn who is teaching the reader by means of this fictional account of the gorilla and his students. That teaching ("...how you came to be the way you are...") is the overarching object of the books and is what engrosses fans so much. But Mr. Quinn never forgets he is writing a novel and maintains an interesting storyline with sympathetic characters throughout. His balance in presenting an account of anthropological history while telling a fantasy story is engaging.

My Ishmael, the sequel to *Ishmael* and *The Story of B*, is a true sequel in that it extends the story of its predecessor. *Ishmael* ended with a finality that would seem to preclude sequels. Staying true to that finality, Mr.

My Ishmael

Quinn set *My Ishmael* in the same time-frame as *Ishmael*, and interleaved its storyline through the gaps. It works.

In *My Ishmael*, Ishmael's pupil is a precocious twelve-year-old girl named Julie Gerchak. We learn, with Julie, the second concept that follows from the one in *Ishmael*. These two concepts are the anchors for Ishmael's teachings.

The first concept is the notion that promoted a particular group of hunter-gathers some 10,000 years ago to begin a campaign of domination over the other hunter-gathers around them. This time period is more generally known as the Agricultural Revolution. Ishmael dubs this campaigning group, the Takers, and avers that their great notion is the Adam and Eve story's "original sin." Further, the Takers' campaign to absorb the surrounding hunter-gathers into settled farming with a controlling hierarchy is allegorically told as the story of Cain and Abel.

The second concept is revealed in *My Ishmael* and is the brilliant idea that allowed the Takers to so effectively impose their life of hierarchy, privileged class, and endless work benefiting the rulers, on the peoples around them (who were living in tribes and hunting and gathering; Ishmael calls them, the Leavers). This Taker idea was extremely effective and continues in effect to this day, dominating the lives of all human beings not still living in tribes on the outskirts of civilization. I'll leave you to discover what that idea is.

This concept of Takers and Leavers is one of the most profound in the books. I find I cannot understand the current world situation outside of referring to this concept. It predicts class struggle and shows capitalism and materialism as natural expressions of the Taker way.

In *My Ishmael* Mr. Quinn presents many ideas and images extending from the Takers-and-Leavers concept. They grabbed me to the point that I made profuse annotations and dog-eared pages as I read through the book (several times). Let me list a few to give an idea of what's there, and include a few criticisms.

This story is an indictment of the Taker lifestyle, which is the lifestyle we are all compelled to live. It starts with a description of Julie's mother to show us where Julie is coming from when she meets Ishmael. Her mother is not a "loser." She's what so many of us are--trying to find happiness in an intolerable life, and not understanding why it's intolerable:

> *...she started putting on weight big time. Luckily, she already had a good job. She heads up the word-processing operation at a big law firm downtown. And then she took to "stopping for a drink after work." This got to be a pretty long stop.*

Ray-views

I can relate. At one point, Ishmael is telling a story where he uses dancing as a metaphor for working. In a beautiful retort to the "work ethic" he has one group of "dancers" say:

We think you're crazy to knock yourselves out dancing fifty and sixty hours a week, but that's your business. If you like it, you do it. But we're not going to do it.

I wish I could say that.

But there is a strand of materialism that runs through the book that I don't care for. Like the part where Ishmael is telling Julie that people can know a lot more than they do, but cultural boundaries keep them from inquiring. They believe that they are "deprived of essential knowledge" and that this knowledge can only be accessed "through supernormal means--prayer, séances, astrology, meditation, past-life reading, channeling, crystal gazing, card reading, and so on." Julie calls this kind of thing, "hoogy-moogy."

While I believe there is truth to what Mr. Quinn is saying through Ishmael here, it's not the whole story. There are good reasons to investigate the paranormal and they're not based on wishful thinking.

There is also a part where Ishmael is using the fighting in Bosnia (going on at the time this book was written) as an example of Takers (us) fighting Leavers who refuse to become Takers. This is a brilliant insight that I think can be applied to many such little wars. But then, referring to Bosnia, he has Ishmael say:

What's happening in that part of the world is merely the latest calamity in a calamitous history that can't be made right by any means whatever.

I've heard that sentiment expressed (far more crudely) many, many times regarding the turmoil on the other side of the world (from the US), and especially in the Middle East. To me, it sounds too much like saying, those are bad and/or crazy people "over there." The truth is, they are violent, when they are violent, often because we (the West) attacked them to steal their resources in our bid to dominate the world. Of course, world events are complex, but it is high delusion to write off the cause as simply being, "they're crazy."

I don't, however, judge this book on these criticisms. They are minor compared to the insight Mr. Quinn offers. It is especially powerful for me when Ishmael talks about our culture's delusions concerning work (our jobs) and our system of education (or lack of the same). The chapter called, *My God, It Isn't Me!*, tells the story of Jeffery, a young man who

My Ishmael

"presented people with a problem," basically because he couldn't bring himself to fit into our Taker culture. I can relate to how he failed to cope, and it makes me wonder about people who we label as, "losers."

I hope I've whetted your curiosity about *My Ishmael* enough to get you to read it. I would, however, recommend you read *Ishmael* first. What is there to find in both books is insight into the human situation, understood from a study of our past. But I warn you, if you approach that study with an open mind, you run the risk of waking from the delusion that our culture ensnares all of us with. And that's just the beginning. When one is so awakened, he or she finds there is a whole new path in front of them, and it can be an unsettling one to follow.

At the book's midpoint, Julie has come to understand the origin of humanity's soul-crushing, Taker cultural prison and asks Ishmael how to break out of it. Ishmael replies:

By refusing to teach your children how to be prisoners.

That's Ishmael's mandate to us--one person at a time changing their minds and determining to live differently and teaching their children that they can do the same.

If you can understand this and commit to the idea, you'll have found the gem buried in this book. Making personal application of this teaching will open you to the potential for a better way, and you'll have found *your* Ishmael.

The Chalice & The Blade

Author: Riane Eisler
Publisher: HarperCollins Publishers
Publication date: 1995
Pages: 304
ISBN-13: 9780062502896
Type: Nonfiction, Social History
Ray's rating: 5 stars

The first version of this review appeared on the www.goodreads.com website in March of 2013.

RAY-VIEW

THE CHALICE & THE BLADE is Riane Eisler's survey of humanity's prehistory from Paleolithic through Neolithic times. It emphasizes the change of our culture from a cooperative, goddess-worshipping society where men and women lived in parity (the Chalice), to a competitive, male-dominated society where women are subjugated (the Blade).

In reviewing our Paleolithic-Neolithic history, Ms Eisler attempts to answer the very fundamental question of "what's wrong with us?" or put in the words of Daniel Quinn (author of *Ishmael*): "Why are things the way they are?"; or as Ms Eisler states the question in *The Chalice & The Blade*:

What is it that chronically tilts us towards cruelty rather than kindness, towards war rather than peace, toward destruction rather than actualization?

The traditional answer is that there is indeed something "wrong with us." Either a defect in the human genome, or a spiritual problem (such as "sin"). Consequently, people are not to be trusted and can only live together in relative peace when a strong government (or other ruling structure) exercises enough force to keep everyone in line (or when acceptance of the right dogma frees people from sin).

In *The Chalice & The Blade*, Ms Eisler avers that the problem is not a defective *us*, but rather a defective *culture* (agreeing with Mr. Quinn, or rather, Mr. Quinn agreeing with her--Ms Eisler said it first). That defect can be pinpointed to a particular time in human history when we began our miserable course to our current troubles:

The Chalice & The Blade

...we see that the roots of our present global crises go back to the fundamental shift in our prehistory that brought enormous changes not only in social structure but also in technology...symbolized by the Blade...

That fundamental shift was the incursion of tribes that had lived on the periphery of the largest concentrations of people on the European land mass (that Ms Eisler calls the Old European societies) around the time of the "Agricultural Revolution" (about 10,000 years ago). These invading peoples (and it was generally a violent invasion) brought with them a new way of living. That way was violent, male-centered in every respect (male gods, etc), and patriarchal. It was pretty much the opposite of the culture it superseded:

All these otherwise widely divergent societies are not only rigidly male dominant but also have a generally hierarchic and authoritarian social structure and a high degree of social violence, particularly warfare.

These invaders are identified by Ms Eisler as the Kurgan--Indo-Europeans who spoke the Aryan language group. Many were from the Caucasus region north of Turkey. They were practitioners of agriculture as much as the Old Europeans, but the society they built around it was based on a might-makes-right philosophy that tended to concentrate the gains of agriculture into the hands of a ruling minority.

The violent ways of the Kurgans made them successful in supplanting the peaceful Old Europeans and the switch to fortified cities in Europe was a result. Another was the legacy of hierarchy and rule-by-force that has plagued humankind since.

Ms Eisler does a great job in the first part of her book in making her case for the peaceful, goddess-worshiping culture of the Paleolithic in Europe. She tells of the vast quantities of feminine figurines, cave art, and the art of Crete, that all speak of societies that honored life as originating with the female. She describes societies of women and men working as equal partners in managing the concerns of settled living for at least tens of thousands of years (with the implication of much longer).

That all ended with the Kurgan invasions, which came in three major waves, wiping out the partnership culture and replacing it with the dominator one.

Ray-views

...the life-giving and nurturing Chalice as the supreme power in the universe has been displaced by the power to dominate and destroy: the lethal power of the Blade. And it is this reality that to our day afflicts all humanity--both women and men.

I think *The Chalice & The Blade* is perceived as a feminist book, and while I think that's true (and is certainly no slight to the book), it is a mistake to see it as that black-and-white. Ms Eisler makes the point that the partnership culture of Old Europe, while it worshiped the Goddess and venerated women, was not simply the opposite to a patriarchal culture. Men were not subservient to women, it's just that women were also not subservient to men. They were, indeed, partners.

So the value in this book, in my opinion, is in its revelation concerning "what happened." It is in its averring that there is nothing wrong with humans, but much that is wrong with the structure of the society impressed on people from the dominator culture that allows no rivals.

Ms Eisler notes that echoes of the partnership culture (she coins the term "gylany" to refer to it) ebb and flow over history, with the better times (for the common people) being when it is at a height in its influence. But the dominator culture (she coins the term "androcracy" to refer to it) always fights back, and today is fighting back especially hard:

Now even nature seems to be rebelling against androcracy...the evidence mounting from every quarter is that the prevailing system is rapidly nearing its logical evolutionary end...What may lie ahead is the final bloodbath of this dying system's violent efforts to maintain its hold.

She makes the "death throes" point several times, but ends with a long section on how much better life will be when the partnership culture returns to prevalence.

But the death throes of androcracy could also be the birth pangs of gylany and the opening of a door into a new future.

I hope so.

Lord of the Flies

Author: William Golding
Publisher: Penguin Group (USA) Incorporated
Publication date: 7/1/1959
Pages: 208
ISBN-13: 9780399501487
Type: Fiction, Psychological Thriller
Ray's rating: 5 stars
Characters: Ralph, Piggy, Roger, Simon, Jack Merridew, Sam and Eric

The first version of this review appeared on the www.goodreads.com website in February of 2014.

RAY-VIEW

HOW deeply ingrained are people's "animal natures?" With all constraints of authority and society removed, how many of us would regress to "savages?" And how quickly? These are the questions dealt with in William Golding's classic 1954 novel, *Lord of the Flies*.

Of course, the word "savage" can carry a certain prejudicial tone, especially if used as a negative or derogatory attribution for tribal peoples. I don't believe, however, that Mr. Golding was trying to paint tribal people as brutish animals in this book. I think he is offering the suggestion that, without civilization, we are all potentially brute animals, or at least, that is true for very many among us. His story is actually more nuanced than that, but it helps to have a feel for how the word "savage" was used in the mid 1950's. For the sake of appreciating this amazing story, consider the word as indicating psychopaths letting loose in all their brutal, sadistic, hierarchical fervor.

So, allowing for that definition, are we savages in suits? Brutes behind cubicles pecking at keyboards?

Lord of the Flies explores that question by stranding a large group of preadolescent boys (the oldest are 12 years old) on a tropical island where there's plenty of food and water, but no adult supervision. They simply must take care of themselves until rescue comes. It all begins as a grand adventure, especially for the older boys, but as the interactions among them become more prompted by needs for food, security, and esteem, their adventure grows dark.

Ray-views

This is certainly a morality play and the three main characters establish the parameters for it. Ralph is the fair-haired hero. He is strong, brave, and smart, though not brilliant. He is moral and has the good sense to realize that building a signal fire on top of the mountain is the most important thing they must do to be rescued. Ralph is quickly designated the boys' leader and elected, "chief."

Ralph's antithesis is Jack Merridew. Jack is the red-haired near-equivalent of Ralph and is already a leader in his own right as head of the choir. His choir-members wear black robes and caps, and maintain their group identity with Jack as their leader. They assume the role of "the hunters" to provide meat from the wild hogs on the island. Jack is readily apparent as the antagonist and the Lucifer symbolism is obvious. His group's role as hunters hearkens to the originators of the "Taker" culture that supplanted hunter-gathers at the Agricultural Revolution, though I expect that reference was not intentional (see Daniel Quinn's *Ishmael*). Jack and Ralph begin as friends but later split as a result of Jack's self-obsession working against Ralph's desire for the common good.

Ralph's main supporter is Piggy. He is very smart, overweight, asthmatic, and badly myopic. Today, we would call him a "geek." We are never told his real name, but he represents a lot of us. He recognizes Ralph as the better person and so supports him over Jack who abuses him (Piggy). Of course, Ralph and nearly everyone else abuses Piggy for being fat and smart, but Piggy can pick his more tolerable degrees of torment. Piggy is Merlin to Ralph's King Arthur and he soon recognizes Jack as Mordred (who was also a kind of Lucifer--smart and handsome and self-absorbed, i.e., proud).

Most people probably take the sense of this story as being that people will digress to "savages" when the constraints of civilization are taken away, but I have to ask if the boys would have digressed to savagery without Jack, who is the catalyst and facilitator for that fall. The run of most people are represented by the "littluns" who follow whoever will provide for them. They are as "good" as whoever is looking out for them. If a savage takes care of them, then they become savages. They abandon civilized mores, represented by the conch, if the savage is ascendant. And those unnoticed little people who are also fervent psychopaths, represented by Roger, will gain power and position if even bigger psychopaths come to power.

There are also secondary characters in *Lord of the Flies* that provide their lessons. Simon is the artist who appreciates beauty and has insight. He is the only character to discover the "beast" for what it is (a dead airman) while everyone else (including, and especially, Jack) imagine it as

Lord of the Flies

a supernatural terror. Simon finds the beauty in the island and personalizes it in his secret hideaway. He remains a supporter of Ralph as much as Piggy does, that is, he remains a supporter of truth and morality but because everyone else does not, he loses.

Then there are the twins, Sam and Eric. They function so much as a single unit, that everyone refers to them as a single person, "Samaneric." Golding does an interesting job in dealing with these twins' bond by having them treated as a single person (even their dialogue is shared between them), although Sam is presented as slightly dominant. Samaneric are an amplification of the littluns. They know that it is morally better to follow Ralph, but when the pressure to follow Jack intensifies, they give in, and self-preservation triumphs.

I especially liked the story's ending. Though a bit implausible in timing, it is literarily brilliant. At the height of the terror that the island has become, it is brought back to "normalcy" in an instant. We are left with the visceral feeling that, in our boring and safe world, savagery lurks just below the surface.

We Wait for the Denouement

Source: Ray's Journal, www.rayfoy.com, 04-May-2014

I RECENTLY purchased three books that I had put on my *Amazon.com* wish-list and they represent a certain path that I want to explore. That path is a consideration of "why things are the way they are." That is, it is an attempt to answer the questions: Why is the world like it is? Why is such ignorant cruelty at work in human affairs? Why does it seem that we are living the Apocalypse? Is there hope for humanity?

Heavy stuff, I realize, but these times call for it. Also, I can't ignore the darker side of reality when it's pressing in on all sides. In fact, everything I've done so far in writing fiction has been my attempt at reconciling, or at least understanding, the good and evil we wrestle with every day. This theme is even in my lighter writings and it would be disingenuous of me to abandon it for the sake of "sounding good" or not offending.

It has long been my desire to ***not*** live in a deluded state that never sees beyond the immediate locus of day-to-day life and accepts the popular beliefs about what's happening in the rest of the world (which is at best based on propaganda and always qualified so as to be safely ignored). This delusion extends into the stories we as a society tell ourselves about who we are and where we come from. For the first two-thirds of my life I pretty much accepted the delusion, or at least, shed it only slowly. Shedding delusions can be painful. The truth revealed is hard to deal with, but once you've seen it, you can't go back.

Let's start with the three books I moved from my wish list to my reading list. They are:

The Story of B by Daniel Quinn

The Chalice & The Blade (Our History, Our Future) by Riane Eisler

Adventures Beyond the Body by William Buhlman

We Wait for the Denouement

I recently finished *The Story of B* and posted my review of it on the Goodreads and BookLikes websites. *The Story of B* is part of Daniel Quinn's *Ishmael* trilogy and I really like that work because it hits an important nail on the head in understanding the antecedents to our current predicament.

Through his teacher characters in his books (especially Ishmael) Mr. Quinn points out that our culture--the one that dominates the world today--had its beginnings in the Neolithic era some 10,000 years ago. It was one among many practicing the domestication of plants and animals and living a settled, agricultural life as opposed to hunting and gathering (foraging). This led to food surpluses, spare time, cities, specialization of labor, and population increases.

This was very nice for humanity. People generally lived longer and better though they (arguably) worked harder. Still, they lived peaceably. Their cities were not fortified and excavations show no signs of martial destruction during this time period. Evidence from their art and funeral practices indicates an equality of the sexes in their societies and even a sophisticated religion of goddess worship (see *The Chalice & The Blade* by Riane Eisler).

Then our ancestors had a bright idea. They decided that they "could have it all" by refusing to follow the law of limited competition. This law is Mr. Quinn's term for a natural law that all life on earth, including humans, followed up until the "agricultural revolution." This law says:

You may compete to the full extent of your capabilities, but you may not hunt down your competitors or destroy their food or deny them access to food.

This law (followed naturally; no committees of cavemen drafted it) allowed animals and people to live sustainably within the bounds of the food resources their environment produced. This is the natural "law of the gods" that allows life on earth to exist in a harmonious balance. Humans came into existence obeying this law and their early cultures are called "Leavers" by Mr. Quinn because they left the rule of the world in the hands of the gods.

Our ancestors' culture (that is, some group of Neolithic people among all the others) decided *they* would take the rule of the world into their own hands. They would be like the gods and Mr. Quinn calls them "Takers." The Takers then began to practice *totalitarian* agriculture where they violated the law of limited competition at every turn. They hunted down their competitors, destroyed their food and denied them access to their food (i.e., they waged total war)--they subdued the earth, were fruitful, and multiplied.

The Taker culture extended their method of totalitarian agriculture to their own people in denying access to food to their own population unless they worked for it (that is, unless they worked for the leaders). This went along with the stratification of society into specialists and managers, and launched the "limitless growth" model. That model was given a tremendous boost by the industrial revolution a couple of hundred years ago. The boost came from the application of fossil fuels to technology that allowed more food production until now when the earth is literally filled up with people and is dying from their wastes.

Mr. Quinn makes a brilliant application of this narrative of human history to the stories in Genesis. The story of the Fall is picture of the emergence of the Taker culture. In eating the fruit of the knowledge of good and evil (abandoning the law of limited competition) Adam and Eve became like the gods (deciding who would live and who would die by practicing totalitarian agriculture), began a life of toil ("the most laborious lifestyle ever practiced on this planet"), and were subject to death (the Taker life "bears with it its own seeds of destruction").

Also the story of Cain and Abel is a picture of the agriculturalist (Cain) killing the herdsman (Abel). They are brothers, but the one took on the power of the gods and decided the other must die. The Takers have been killing the Leavers for ten thousand years.

This is basically the picture presented by Mr. Quinn in his *Ishmael* books describing why the world is like it is and why we've reached this point. I would add that the Taker culture (called "dominator" by Riane Eisler), with its emphasis on hierarchy and acquisition of power, rewards psychopathic behavior. So the premise that "the world is run by psychopaths" gains much credence.

Riane Eisler's, *The Chalice & The Blade,* agrees with the basic premises of Mr. Quinn's books. From both, it is easy to see the impetus of Taker culture that has brought us right through the limits of growth to the climax of Taker (and human) history. We are living that climax now with some fearsome punctuating events (war, famine, police states, etc) and the promise of more. We wait for the denouement to reveal whether the result will be a world collapsed to a sustainable level, or a world extinct of all life.

What Happened to Us?

Source: Ray's Journal, www.rayfoy.com, 01-Jun-2014

"WHAT HAPPENED?" is a natural question, a nearly automatic question, when you come upon a scene of destruction, extreme disorder, or just something that is obviously not right. It's the question begged when a bad result is seen with no obvious cause (like the proverbial train wreck).

The books I have examined so far in our literary expedition (*The Story of B, The Chalice & The Blade*) have centered around this question as applied to the sight of the current condition of human Industrial-Technical civilization. The loss of freedom by peoples around the world (especially in the US), the suffering caused by extreme weather aberrations (natural and human-made), the extreme disparities in living conditions between the haves and have-nots (wealth inequalities), the promulgation of open-ended war, the rise of brutal political extremes, the depletion of fossil fuels, and the economic collapse of the "first world" are elements of the (impending) scene of destruction to be explained. That explanation is these books' primary theme and concern.

These books tell us that humanity's problem is that it is, indeed, fallen. This fall, however, is a matter of culture. It was a change in the overriding structure of the beliefs and directions that govern people. This change was from one of peaceful equalitarianism and partnering relations among people (and among the sexes), to one of domination (by the males over women and by one group over another) and competitive hierarchy. This change was (to use Daniel Quinn's terms) from a culture of Leavers (leaving world rule to the gods) to one of Takers (taking world rule from the gods).

The authors of these books (Daniel Quinn and Riane Eisler) indicate that there is no flaw within human beings, but rather, the flaw is in the Taker (or dominator) culture that is the prevalent culture over all the earth. In fact, Quinn makes quite a point of this, especially in *My Ishmael*. But if that be so, then why has humanity remained in thrall of the Taker culture--a culture oppressive of most humans and destructive to the earth-

-for some ten thousand years? I believe, as I noted in previous journal entries, it is because the Taker culture rewards and promotes psychopaths. So, generally, those at the top of the pyramid are the worst of us, and they now have the power and the tools to keep the rest of us (though greater in number) under control.

But the arrogance and God-complex of these ruling elites (declaring with Lucifer: "I will ascend above the heights of the clouds; I will make myself like the Most High") has reached a point of destructiveness such that life on earth may not survive. Ms Eisler saw this some twenty years ago:

What may lie ahead is the final bloodbath of this dying system's violent efforts to maintain its hold.

And this is the point in our journey that looks most bleak to me. I see the oligarchs that rule the world as fighting hard against the limits of growth heralded by the depletion of cheap fossil fuels and sheer overpopulation. They have very powerful tools now, powerful enough to take us all down with them, and that seems to be their intent. They are still eating of that fruit of that Tree of the Knowledge of Good and Evil, imagining themselves as gods, and deciding who lives and who dies.

At this point, I could go down a very dark road, indeed, but I will not do that. I want to travel a higher road.

In writing my *Dentville* novels, I am envisioning a time beyond this present darkness. I see us as having made it, and being forced to face the consequences of the long reign of Taker culture and living at a much simpler level (that I believe will be at a roughly Neolithic level). Our fight at that time will be against the resurgence of the Taker culture.

So if humanity survives, it will be because of a brightening of a light from our higher natures to a point of prevalence, perhaps aided by Gaia herself.

In *Dentville*, the spiritual beliefs of people, especially as expressed through the sages and the Order of Gaia, are based on folk beliefs as I understand them. The sages in my stories are shamans, working as liaisons between people in the physical life, and the spirits. People struggle through this physical existence with hardship and fear, and look to what's beyond to provide meaning and support. We'll need that as we go on, struggling into our future.

Suggested for Further Reading

Bury My Heart at Wounded Knee: An Indian History of the American West by Dee Brown

Guns, Germs, and Steel by Jared Diamond

Collapse by Jared Diamond

Ray-views

On Prophecy

MY ATTITUDE towards the subject of prophecy has blown hot and cold over my life. When I was young, I held the same view as my fundamentalist Protestant peers of believing every word of Bible prophecy (i.e., the Biblical prophets were all inspired by God and therefore inerrant, especially where predictions about Jesus' birth and about the End Times were concerned). As a teenager, I read and reread Hal Lindsey's book, *The Late Great Planet Earth*, until I knew that evangelical tome's future timeline by heart and took it for gospel. In my opinion, any prophecies outside the Bible were "fortune telling" and either fraudulent or satanic. In my post-evangelical, materialistic phase, I rejected all prophesying and any existence beyond the physical. In my later years, I rediscovered a higher plane of spirituality and became open again to the idea of people with psychic abilities being able to see the future. I didn't give the subject deep consideration, however, until I sort of stumbled onto reading John Hogue's books.

I became aware of John Hogue from seeing him on History Channel specials about Nostradamus. Mr. Hogue is a recognized scholar of Nostradamus' life and predictions, and he is nearly always called upon for comment when documentaries about the famous seer are made. He is also a seer himself, using astrology as his chief tool for prognostication. A few years ago, I listened to an interview of him by Whitley Strieber and was so impressed with his knowledge of current events that I subscribed to his newsletter. I also purchased some of his books and did reviews on them. Consequently, the books reviewed in this category are all his.

While I have become open to a wide range of spiritual ideas, I have not really considered prophecy or precognition terribly seriously until recently. I have had readings by New Orleans fortune-tellers and found newspaper horoscopes that were amazingly "right on." Gradually, I've come to a certain consideration of the accuracy of inspired predictions. I mean, people talk about the percentage of correct predictions made by various prognosticators, historical and current, with the implication that the greater the number of "hits," the greater the validity of the seer. But surely such validity is not a function of percentage of hits. Would not any number of correct predictions beyond the expected average for guessing indicate some transcendent aspect of physical reality worth investigating? It seems to me that introspection and some open-minded research answers this question in the affirmative.

I've mentioned *The Late Great Planet Earth* and, while it's not scholarly research by any means, it is instructional for seekers. It is a screed of Protestant, fundamentalist thought on eschatology that was "scary" to believers in the 1970s. The reason it was, is what makes it interesting. Because it was "Biblical" prophecy, fundamentalist Christians accepted it where they condemned the writings of astrologers and anyone who claimed inspired knowledge of the future by any other means. It is that belief that is the interesting point here. Especially in the US "Bible Belt," where belief in Bible Prophecy was taken for granted and the only question was whether Mr. Lindsey was interpreting it correctly. Most believers thought he was; enough for him to build a career on his ideas.

Hal Lindsey tapped into what I consider a subset of "folk" belief in the supernatural. Segueing from there you find a widespread belief in spiritualism (or mysticism) among "common folk" that is largely not acknowledged as such by them. I believe it's there, however, based on seeing many people accept the reality of ghostly phenomena and mediumship. I find the works of John Edward, George Anderson, and other psychic mediums compelling and indicative of a transcendent reality (see the Foreword in my book of short fiction, *The Wider World*) and they have a significant following among regular people. Whitley Strieber's writings also are valuable in studying transcendent phenomena. I haven't reviewed these authors (except for Mr. Strieber; see the "Beyond the Usual" category) but I've read their works and they inform my reviews and this essay.

So there is a popular belief in things spiritual and supernatural that puts credence in prophecies. So what shall we make of this? If there is a reality to "seeing the future," what is its nature and how does it work? I think that, somewhere, spirit communications and precognition (Extrasensory Perception; ESP) collide in explaining this phenomena, though I can't say how.

Years ago, I bought a little book, that I recently reread, that considers cases of precognition. It's called, *Riddle of the Future* by Andrew MacKenzie. It's out of print now, but you can still find it by Internet search (as of this writing you can get used copies through Amazon.com from third parties). It is a casebook of events that seem to be instances of seeing the future and the author takes a scientific approach in evaluating them. He draws a lot from the writings of members of the British Society for Psychic Research (SPR) which spans largely from the late nineteenth

On Prophecy

to mid twentieth centuries (and even up to the 1970s). His observations on these cases, and his quotes of SPR members, offer much to consider in the workings of prophecy that I find echoed in Mr. Hogue's works. For example:

> ...*while the course of future events appears to have been foreseen, these events are not inexorably fixed but are capable of being modified by deliberate action beforehand...the future foreseen is what might, and most probably would happen if things were left to run their course...* (MacKenzie quoting H. F. Saltmarsh from *Foreknowledge*)

It is a strong tenet that prophecies are not "set in stone" (in opposition to the common belief about Bible prophecies and the premise of Greek tragedies). But even if precognitions are malleable, why do we sense them at all? Mr. MacKenzie theorizes that they may come from some kind of disturbance in time. That is, an event at a given point in time (say, the Titanic sinking or the JFK assassination) might create "waves" of cognition that produce a weak effect earlier in time that sensitives pick up. It may be sort of like, as Mr. MacKenzie says, when you wake up before the alarm clock goes off.

Mr. MacKenzie also implies that spirit communication may be responsible for at least some precognitions. He notes a time period of some thirty years, beginning in 1901, when several thousands "scripts" were produced from numerous spirit communications (such as automatic writing) that were precognitive in nature when compared to one another. One theme of the scripts was world war, predicting the first and second, as well as a third (which also a theme of the prophecies by Nostradamus and other seers expounded on in Mr. Hogue's writings).

I can see the conjectures of *Riddle of the Future* as applying to the books I've reviewed in this category. What are prophecies but precognitions? I guess you could get technical and define them as sets of precognitions and then get into whether they are "revealed" (by a higher being or discarnate humans) or "perceived" (picking up on those time disturbances). In any case, they are sightings of future events by people throughout human history who were sensitive to doing such, for whatever reason. Very likely, it is a capability of most anyone who settles their mind, concentrates, and tries. And it seems various tools aid the various sensitives--astrology, tarot cards, palm reading, Ouija boards, automatic writing, and so on.

So there is a strong case, I think, for the reality of future-seeing based on evidence (if not "proof") and experience (very many more people

Ray-views

experience such phenomena than admit it). Again, Mr. MacKenzie says it well:

> *It is not that the evidence for it is weak, but that people find it particularly hard to conceive of precognition as being a reality...that we find something inconceivable may only indicate an unfortunate limitation in our powers of conceiving.*

    This is the background against which I read and reviewed the works of John Hogue in this category. It includes three books of predictions that focus on the immediately following years (relative to the time of this writing--2015) and that mostly concern world political events. I refer you to my Ray-views and to the books themselves for specifics. One book expounds on the Hopi Prophecies, which have gotten a lot of attention lately and I see them referred to quite often. Another is an overview of the life and prophecies of Nostradamus. This work seems to validate a lot of *Riddle of the Future* with the famous quatrains being strong indications of what might be if we don't do something. Mr. Hogue indicates that he thinks many (if not most) of the quatrains (predictions) didn't come to pass because circumstances changed and/or people made decisions that altered the predicted outcome.

    So prophecies can be thought of as warnings. Their subjects are usually either mundane or alarming (wars, famine, death, and other disasters), and rarely hopeful. Since this is a time of converging calamities that seem to presage human extinction (or at least a strong possibility for such), it seems only prudent to examine the precognitions of seers, past and present, who have a track record that indicates validity. Compared to one another, they may offer warnings we desperately need to hear.

    At this perilous time in human history, we need a clue.

The Essential Hopi Prophecies

Author: John Hogue
Publisher: HogueProphecy Publishing
Publication date: 06/19/2015
Pages: 58
ASIN: B0102X29CQ
Type: Nonfiction, Prophecy
Ray's rating: 5 stars

The first version of this review appeared on the www.booklikes.com and www.amazon.com websites in June of 2015.

RAY-VIEW

IT SEEMS a trend these days that commentaries and essays about current world events quote the prophecies of the Hopi Indians. They do so with good reason and this behooves the serious seeker to look into who these people are and what they have to say. *The Essential Hopi Prophecies* by John Hogue is a very good place to begin that inquiry.

In seven chapters written in readable, engaging prose, Mr. Hogue gives us an overview of the Hopi as a pueblos-dwelling indigenous people, living in the "Four Corners" region of the US southwest. In their millennia of living there, they produced a folklore that contains stories of three previous "worlds" (which I take to be instances of world civilizations) that reached their zeniths of development and then perished. It also contains predictions concerning the destruction of the fourth world (our world) followed by the birth of a fifth. This coming death-rebirth for humanity is known by the Hopi as "The Great Purification."

These predictions for The Great Purification are the main concern of *The Essential Hopi Prophecies* and Mr. Hogue expounds upon them with skills gleaned from long experience at interpreting prophecy. For instance, he draws from his knowledge of Nostradamus and Mattias Stormberger to make a compelling case for the Hopi predicting a nuclear-powered World War III. But even without interpretation, what I find remarkable about these prophecies is their relatively unambiguous language. For example, a *Gourd of Ashes* along with: *"The white brother will bring the symbol of the Sun, which makes a great explosion shaking the Earth,"* sounds a lot like a nuclear explosion. And then descriptions of the Sun, the Swastika and the

Ray-views

Red, are readily seen as an allusion to the World War II conflict between the West and Japan, Nazi Germany, and Communist Russia.

Interpreting such images, Mr. Hogue is able to present a list of signs that the Hopi say will precede the Great Purification. These include atomic bomb drops, World War II, the telegraph (mass communications), trains (rapid transportation), cobwebs in the sky (indicating air travel but more specifically, in my opinion, artifacts of geoengineering), and even the obtaining of rocks from the moon and human residence in a "teepee in the sky" (the international space station). There are other signs that Mr. Hogue deals with at some length, like the blue star that "falls with a great crash." This one is not as straightforward as others and so Mr. Hogue gives us some speculations as to its meaning.

Another sign is "*a great red power wearing a red cloak will come by a road in the air from the east.*" This has been interpreted, apparently by the Hopi themselves, as an influx of Buddhist thought from red-robed practitioners into western countries (including the American southwest). Mr. Hogue makes a good case for this being indicative of the Tibetan diaspora from Chinese oppression. He also makes an interesting case for the prophecy alluding to the followers of Bhagwan Shree Rajneesh (an Indian mystic also called Osho) who built a commune in Oregon (Mr. Hogue has some personal experience with that bit of history).

Other topics touched on in the book include a discussion of the Hopi "Prophecy Rock" that expresses male-female potentials in a sense that reminds me of similar thought in Daniel Quinn and Riane Eisler's books. Then there's a section on fulfilled Native American prophecies, centering on the coming of the white man. And there's a discussion on various messianic traditions in the folklore of indigenous American peoples. Such traditions that touch on, and even arguably transcend, classic western thought, belie Hollywood images of "savage Indians," though Mr. Hogue's essay on the Thanksgiving Day holiday (Chapter 4) might indicate they were not so much "savage" as "pissed off."

As you can see, there's a lot of ground covered in this little book. Even so, it's not an exhaustive text, but is rather a launching pad that can take the seeker down a number of enlightening paths. A lot of the material is based on previous works by Mr. Hogue and he refers to those via links in the text. They are good paths to follow in your studies along with *Book of the Hopi* by Frank Waters, which Mr. Hogue quotes.

We live in a time of converging calamities bearing towards a near-future that even nonreligious people see as apocalyptic. People seem to sense this even as they deny it with actions that say "tomorrow will be like today." The fear that tomorrow may actually be different, even much

The Essential Hopi Prophecies

worse, prompts us to look for some sane direction through the anticipated storm. So we turn to what seers have written through the ages, looking for clues to help. Among that literature, the Hopi prophecies stand out as especially deserving of our attention. *The Essential Hopi Prophecies* will point you to them.

The Essential Nostradamus

Author: John Hogue
Publisher: HogueProphecy Publishing
Publication date: 09/11/2014
Pages: 137
ASIN: B00NJ898Z8
Type: Nonfiction, Prophecy
Ray's rating: 5 stars

The first version of this review appeared on the www.goodreads.com and www.amazon.com websites in November of 2014.

RAY-VIEW

THE ESSENTIAL NOSTRADAMUS by John Hogue is an excellent treatment of just what the title implies. In very readable prose, Mr. Hogue provides a concise survey of the French prophet's life, his theory and methods for divination, a methodology for interpretation of the quatrains, interpretations of some of Nostradamus' best known predictions from the past (his future), the present, and the far future. There's also a chapter about a "man from the East" who represents a ray of hope among otherwise really dark predictions. Overall, the book is an intelligent, engaging introduction to the life and work of the Renaissance era seer born Michel de Nostredame.

The book starts with a synopsis of Nostradamus' life story and it's probably the lightest reading in the whole work. Mr. Hogue gives us a feel for who Nostradamus was from birth to death. He shows us the prophet as a precocious youth who impressed his grandfathers enough to begin tutoring him, and later enroll him in a liberal arts education and then medical school. We are taken through his years as a young doctor fighting the bubonic plague (or *le Charbon*, in the old French), losing his first wife and children to it, and to some years of wandering afterwards, in part, to avoid the Inquisition. But it was when he began publishing his prophecies that Nostradamus gained fame as a seer. These earned him the patronage of Catherine de Medici (the French queen) and he subsequently became very popular in French courts. In the last years of his life, Catherine made him "Counselor and Physician in Ordinary," a title with privilege and salary.

The Essential Nostradamus

With some idea of who Nostradamus was, Mr. Hogue then tells us something of how he went about his divinations and the ancient texts he drew from. He shows us Nostradamus studying ancient works on "Egyptian, Chaldaean and Assyrian magic rituals" and the "occult works attributed to the biblical King Solomon." With this knowledge as his guide, Nostradamus would ascend the steps to his secluded study, enter a circle of lit candles, and meditate over a boiling cauldron of herbs. Entering into a trance or meditative state, he would receive his visions of the future from the spirits (ranked as angels, daemons, elemental spirits, etc--the implication being that Nostradamus' predictions ultimately came from the "other side").

Before delving into the prophecies themselves, Mr. Hogue gives us some instruction on understanding them. Nostradamus' predictions are composed as four-line poems that are highly symbolic and even obscure. This was intentional on Nostradamus' part, "so that the ignorant and prejudiced would deem him a fool and leave him alone, while the more open minded might pass beyond the verbal roadblocks..." So some guidance from a scholar is needed to understand them.

Mr. Hogue begins his considerations of the better known of Nostradamus' predictions with the one describing the death of King Henry II of France (published some five years or so before the event). He shows us how Nostradamus' symbols and language point to the event. In this case, there's not much room for speculation about meanings, but in the other predictions, especially those of the far future, there is greater symbology with alternate possibilities and Mr. Hogue takes us through those. Such is the pattern through the rest of the book.

Mr. Hogue presents the prophecies in four chapters, dealing with predictions of the past, present, and future (with respect to our time) and one chapter devoted to the appearance of a special spiritual leader or teacher ("man from the East") in our time (or thereabouts). In them all, Mr. Hogue points out Nostradamus' symbology, use of anagrams, classical allusions, lack of sequence, etc, and then deciphers what they are saying.

Even so, many of the prophecies remain obscure and open to multiple interpretations. Mr. Hogue acknowledges this and makes the point that genuine prophecy points to possible futures that can be altered if people change their behavior and make wiser, or at least different, decisions. He says that of all Nostradamus' prophecies, "over 800 are little more than augury-babble" but he also believes that "...many of the incomprehensible quatrains are accurate chronicles of events that "might have been" if history had taken a different turn..." This is an important point in considering any prophetic work.

In these "essential" prophecies of Nostradamus we see, even within the constraints of symbols and alternate scenarios, a bleak picture painted of humanity's future. How could it be otherwise? Human history is a pretty bleak recounting since at least the Agricultural Revolution. The future will surely be more of the same, and even more dire; unless we come to our senses and change it. This is the message of Nostradamus' prophecies and of Mr. Hogue's book, which I highly recommend.

Kamikaze Tomorrowland

Author: John Hogue
Publisher: HogueProphecy Publishing on Smashwords
Publication date: 2013
Pages: 14
Type: Fiction, Science Fiction & Fantasy
Ray's rating: 5 stars

The first version of this review appeared on the www.amazon.com website in October of 2013.

RAY-VIEW

KAMIKAZE TOMORROWLAND is a well-structured little tale that involves a movement through time (though not exactly hardcore SF "time travel") and resolves the time-traveler's dilemma of contradiction in a very pleasing way.

I don't want to make this review a spoiler and the story is very short, so I won't go much into plot. It does begin in World War II with a Kamikaze pilot on his last mission. Akio Sarazawa is flying his Zero fighter over the ocean looking for the US fleet. He considers his past and his certain future as he flies. He is especially concerned with what death will be like for him. The answer to that is greatly unexpected, and launches events that convey the point of the story.

Mr. Hogue relates Akio's experiences in a voice that is believable for the actions and settings. He gives just enough technical information on WWII combat flying to work for a story of this length, showing he did his research. And he's enough of a SF fan to know how to construct such a story that is appealing to other SF fans.

Mr. Hogue uses images well (joystick, rosary, Buddhist talisman, *Kimigayo*) as well as themes that give the story some depth--the futility of war, the futility of dying for a political cause (or at least, for a political/religious personality). His economy of words is also admirable. The story is some 5800 words but they are enough to convey that Akio's main prompt to become a Kamikaze was peer pressure combined with convincing propaganda. There's enough flashback to see his early, favorable connection to the United States and how that was marred by the napalm raids that killed his parents. Still, we get the feeling that his fight and self-sacrifice were not based so much on hate, as on a manipulated patriotism (i.e., love of emperor). It is an underscore of war's futility.

Had this been all the good in *Kamikaze Tomorrowland*, I would have rated it 4 stars. But it was the extra dimension of the story that earned it a fifth star from me.

John Hogue is a scholar of prophecy and a prognosticator in his own right. He is an authority on the life and writings of Nostradamus and you'll often see him in documentaries about the French seer. He is a prolific writer on this subject and produces e-books on predictions for the coming year, every year. *Kamikaze Tomorrowland* is his attempt to extend his prophetic work into fiction. He describes the result as a new genre in science fiction he calls, "ScryFy." In his own words:

> *I define Scry-Fy as a form of prophecy-science fiction and fantasy. It is neither fiction nor non-fiction. Scry-Fy is transfix-tion. 'Scrying' is a basic form of divination using objects that, in the hand of the initiate, can reflect the dark shadows of potential future destiny.*

I've read enough of Mr. Hogue's writings and heard him in interviews to have an understanding of how he views prophecy and I see that view in *Kamikaze Tomorrowland*. In a nutshell, it seems to be that energies build in the numinous and physical worlds that lead to events that can be descried before they happen by the "initiate" tapping into those energies. Very often, what is seen are the potentialities for events (and consequences) more so than "this will happen at this time." The scrying process can produce insight as to courses to follow to avert or diminish an adverse future.

Kamikaze Tomorrowland avers this idea in its plot, and in summation in Akio Sarazawa's words:

> ...*I found myself at the crossroads of life and death. I was shown what might have been if...*

Read *Kamikaze Tomorrowland* to get the full impact of Akio's words in light of this view of prophecy, and to understand why great teachers teach with parables.

Ten Predictions for 2015

Author: John Hogue
Publisher: HogueProphecy Publishing
Publication date: 12/19/2015
Pages: 45
ASIN: B00R9WD54K
Type: Nonfiction, Prophecy
Ray's rating: 5 stars

The first version of this review appeared on the www.goodreads.com, and www.amazon.com websites in January of 2015.

RAY-VIEW

TEN PREDICTIONS FOR 2015 is John Hogue's prelude to his much larger work, *Predictions 2015-2016*, in much the same way that the year 2015 is prelude to a much larger time in human history.

Ten Predictions is a short work at 45 pages but much information and thought food is packed in that small space. The first section of the book is the ten predictions. They are numbered and written as essays of varying lengths. They are not so much a listing of discrete predictions as they are themes and event directions that support one another and build a picture of the times ahead.

The overarching theme in all the predictions is that *2015 is the year of last chances*--economically, politically, and ecologically. Changes must be made in the coming year to forestall dark consequences. For instance, we need to change our economic model from an imaginary one (fiat currency) to something value-based to avoid a "Greater Depression."

Mr. Hogue also sees 2015 as a beginning of trends that lead to a changed world. He sees a shift in world political power from West (US/NATO) to East as the BRICS nations rise from the fall of the petrodollar.

He sees a rising populist movement spurred by technology that topples (or greatly weakens) the power of central authorities.

He says a lot concerning war in our future, but indicates some nuances about how it unfolds depending on decisions made soon. He sees (based on some specifics from Nostradamus) a war in the Persian Gulf involving the US, Israel, and Iran (with a last-minute chance to avoid it).

Ray-views

He sees tensions with Russia leading to a nuclear standoff over Ukraine, though just short of war.

Most interesting among these themes and directions are some specifics. For instance, he sees an implementation of technology in the form of a "black box" that will provide household energy independence. He sees the Internet morphing to (or augmented by) a base of cell phone connections and so surviving attempts by authority to control it. He sees a "World War Green" that will be pretty much an "anti-war."

And he offers some prophetic indications of the winner of the 2016 US presidential election that includes one who has "a destiny to become president unless..."

After the predictions, Mr. Hogue includes an essay entitled, "The Future of Richness." Actually, it's a talk he gave to a gathering of some very rich people (that he considered to be among the 1%) upon their invitation. It's largely about Mr. Hogue's time with his guru, Osho. Since Osho was sometimes called "The Rich Man's Guru," that recounting was probably germane to his audience. The talk does relate to this book's prophetic theme, however, in that it ends with an encouragement for these rich folk to find the enlightenment to use their wealth and resources to lead humanity into a better future.

The book's last section contains sample chapters from some of Mr. Hogue's previous works. These are:

A New Cold War: The Prophecies of Nostradamus, Stormberger, and Edgar Cayce

Nostradamus: The End of End Times

Nostradamus: A Life and Myth

The samples add value to this book by supporting it with some interesting predictions and accounts of fulfilled prophecies. Notable is the prediction of the rise of a new spiritual teacher from the east that is gleaned from Buddhist, Hindu, and Christian writings. Also, there is an account of the *real* prediction Nostradamus made concerning 9-11.

Ten Predictions for 2015 is an appetizer for *Predictions 2015-2016*. But it's a tasty appetizer that will give Mr. Hogue's fans the scholarly interpretation of past prophets using the clever prose they've come to expect from him. And I highly recommend it to anyone who is looking with open mind for prophetic insights into these turbulent and momentous times.

Predictions 2015-2016

Author: John Hogue
Publisher: HogueProphecy Publishing
Publication date: 04/24/2015
Pages: 384
ASIN: B00WONOGAG
Type: Nonfiction, Prophecy
Ray's rating: 5 stars

The first version of this review appeared on the www.booklikes.com and www.amazon.com websites in May of 2015.

RAY-VIEW

PREDICTIONS 2015-2016 is seer and prophecy scholar John Hogue's description of what's in store for the world based on his research of contemporary events, astrological readings, and insights offered by his "oracle." It provides a good overview of the status of world events, governments, economies, and climate for the time period specified and beyond. That overview stays true to the *Predictions* part of the title in that it contains accounts of what will happen, and of what can happen, based on choices made in this prophetically significant time. Those choices and outcomes are further illuminated by passages of prophetic writings from past seers--Nostradamus foremost among them.

In this book, as in his other written works, Mr. Hogue uses astrology as his chief tool for prognostication. Consequently, you get passages like:

"It sits at 21 degrees Scorpio in the Twelfth House, conjoined Venus and my Ascendant at 20 degrees."

Don't be daunted by that, though, because most such passages aren't so astrologically technical and Mr. Hogue provides layman explanations for those that are. This doesn't detract from the book's message. It even enhances it in much the same way a book involving sailing ships might use nautical terms and so provide a salty ambiance for its story (re: *Two Years Before the Mast*).

You also don't have to "believe in astrology" to get the value of this book. I've long thought that people sensitive to the supra-dimensional aspect of reality (i.e., "psychics") usually have some kind of tool such as

Ray-views

astrology, the tarot, palm-reading, Ouija boarding, etc, to facilitate their access to the numinous. Mr. Hogue seems to endorse this idea when, in regard to the operational influence on human activities by the stars and planets, he says:

"Perhaps they have no direct influence on humanity at all, but they inspire the seer like a catalyst."

If you are open to this view, then you will obtain the optimum value from *Predictions 2015-2016* and Mr. Hogue's inspiration. And that value covers a lot of ground. In twelve chapters and an epilogue, Mr. Hogue touches on most of the events, momentums, and situations operating in the world today. For each, he offers an overview of its history and current status, relates the astrological perspective, and adds any further word on the subject from his oracle. He then offers his predictions, which may be a declarative statement of what he believes will happen ("I predict that..."), or his view of what trends will develop, or what the choices are and their potential consequences.

Without giving anything away, the areas covered in the book include the fate of the American Empire (and the potentiality of nuclear war with Russia), world economy and the control of it by global corporations and their "trade deals," a future defined by decentralization in technology and politics, the 2016 US presidential election and its likely winner, an American rebellion against the 1% police state, EU hubris and Greek economic problems, the possibilities for a "blood" pandemic, the BRICS challenge to the West, conflict stemming from the crisis in Ukraine, Middle East issues including the rise of ISIS, and global warming leading to climate change with all its miseries.

These are heavy subjects and contemplating them honestly can be depressing. Mr. Hogue acknowledges this in his introduction and promises the reader that his book will not sugar-coat any of it:

"Numerous almanacs and forecasts for 2015 are available that will mollify you, that will "Mary Poppins" to you this bitter pill of a year with a spoon full of sugary BS to make the medicine go down. This book won't do that."

And it doesn't. Even so, Mr. Hogue's prose is characteristically witty with a liberal and unapologetic use of insightful puns scattered throughout. He even alters his "voice" from street-slang to poetic, as he deems fit, to make his points. It often includes re-worded popular songs. All this adds a lightness to keep the subject matter from becoming so dark

Predictions 2015-2016

that it gets overwhelming, and it helps carry readers along through the book's expansive list of topics.

Now, the potential problem with a book of predictions is that it can be viewed simply as a game where the predictions are compiled and checked for accuracy to produce a "score." A high score might earn the author the title of "pretty good predictor," where a low score might lead to a dismissal of the book and anything else the author says. While such "scoring" is possible, it is secondary, especially in this book where so many important issues are discussed with candor and buttressed with careful research. I recommend that readers think past "scoring" and consider what Mr. Hogue says about things like the potential for nuclear war erupting from the Ukraine and Iran situations, or the threat of human extinction from global warming.

Predictions 2015-2016 is a book written for a specific time. Mr. Hogue says in the introduction that that time is one of "last chances." Humanity must make some critical decisions, now, to facilitate a much needed restart. This time will feel, he says, "something like death is approaching...to be supplanted by the unfamiliar, the new." And further, "A birth is coming out of this death." This book should help you see the fitful death coming for nations, systems, and grooves of thought that have run their course, before there is a birth of anything better.

I try not to do spoilers in my reviews so I have not given here much of Mr. Hogue's conclusions or specific predictions. I urge you to make those discoveries for yourself by reading *Predictions 2015-2016* and I predict that, if you do so with an open mind and honest desire to learn, you'll be richly rewarded. But I warn you: never mind looking at the future, even looking honestly at the present is not a task for the fainthearted. Seeing things as they are is tough and can lead to despair.

Mr. Hogue addresses this issue of reality-prompted despair in his book's epilogue, which is by itself, worth the cost of the book. Its impact is loaded by the preceding twelve chapters so don't skip right to it. You should read the book chapter-by-chapter, taking in what is said in each, and then meditatively read the epilogue. That exercise will, in my opinion, bring you to the closest facility for hope that I can find in this dark age, and so help you face the future.

Predictions for the Last Blood Moon

Author: John Hogue
Publisher: HogueProphecy Publishing
Publication date: 07/31/2015
Pages: 66
ASIN: B013509FBM
Type: Nonfiction, Prophecy
Ray's rating: 5 stars

The first version of this review appeared on the www.booklikes.com, www.goodreads.com, and www.amazon.com websites in August of 2015.

RAY-VIEW

  IN HIS *Predictions for the Last Blood Moon*, prophecy scholar John Hogue reviews the portents he has noted for the first three Blood Moon events, and then describes what world shifts and potentials will be unleashed by the fourth. In the process, he discusses the current hoopla surrounding the Blood Moons and contrasts the religious, dogmatic interpretation of Biblical prophecy with the scholarly, open-minded sort.
  Blood moons are total lunar eclipses. The "blood" designation comes from the moon being illuminated by sunlight in the red wavelength, as refracted through earth's atmosphere, at the point of totality. That is, the moon takes on a red color at the height of a total eclipse. When this happens four times in a row, each separated by six full moons and with no partial eclipses in between, it's called a tetrad.
  This book's tone is Mr. Hogue's usual blend of scholarly discussion, no-holds-barred commentary, and points made with yoga-like-twisting word-play and irreverent humor. For example, in reference to a red moon eclipse, he says:

  "Is she going menstrual—"turning to blood" as some dire and unclean portent of the Lord God on the rag, reckoning a final day of judgment and doom upon mankind?"

  And when discussing the tendency of people to assign dire meaning to indifferent events, he says:

Predictions for the Last Blood Moon

"Omens are the "oh!" of men projecting alarm on innocent and natural phenomena."

Such passages provide levity to guide the reader through some heavy material.

Because the term, "blood moon," is derived from a passage in the Old Testament Book of Joel that is considered prophetic, the recent (as of this writing) tetrad has been seized upon by the fundamentalist crowd as being a sign from God that portends events leading to the Second Coming. Mr. Hogue reviews this idea in some detail in the Introduction, noting it's descent from the writings of Hal Lindsey (*The Late Great Planet Earth*) in the 1970s to current tomes by John Hagee, Rev Mark Blitz, and (I'm sure) many others.

Mr. Hogue dissects the narrow, "Bible-based" fundamentalist assertions (especially Hagee's) in the light of his own broader-based studies of prophecy. He points out Hagee's errors in Biblical and historical interpretation, and notes that Hagee's book (*Four Blood Moons*) is more about supporting dogma than about relating fact or discovering new truth.

In noting motivations for the sheer business success of Hagee and others, Mr. Hogue says:

"Their recipe for success : cook up a thick stew of hubris, hope and fears in religious pot boilers based on a watered-down broth of badly translated Greek, Aramaic and Hebrew ancient texts."

The problem with this fundamentalist, end-times stew is that the ardent partakers of it tend to direct us to a bad place (and some of them are government leaders, and they do seem to dominate the US military). As Mr. Hogue says:

"In my view, such Christian theologians along with their Jewish and Islamic counterparts all unconsciously promote a dogmatic eschatological dream that drags the Middle East, and perhaps the whole world, down into their apocalyptic nightmare without any salvation waiting at the end as anticipated reward."

Such words will offend fervent fundamentalists and Mr. Hogue has already tussled with them on his website. There's no getting around that, though, especially if you're to address Biblical material honestly. *Predictions for the Last Blood Moon*, in my opinion, does just that.

In regards to actual prophetic implications of the Blood Moons, Mr. Hogue uses his tool of astrology to evaluate them. In chapters for each

Ray-views

Blood Moon of the tetrad, he examines the associated positions of the sun and stars, and the strength of astrological "windows of influence" in force at the time. What he finds are the directions in play for world events that the Blood Moons underscore. These are, in a nutshell:

1st Blood Moon: 15-Apr-2014
"Nationalistic impulses" prompt renewed violence in Ukraine between the NATO-backed Kiev government and the Russian-backed Donbass fighters.

2nd Blood Moon: 08-Oct-2014
The Syrian Civil War spills over into Iraq in the form of an "invasion" by the ISIS group. This prompts a return of American "advisers" to Iraq.

3rd Blood Moon: 04 Apr 2015
The US and Iran put together a framework for an agreement on Iran's nuclear program, and later the deal itself is brokered (on Jul 14). But the "deal" is a bad one for Iran (they get some sanctions lifted but lose most all control of their nuclear program and open an invasive door to the west). Unbiased observers think there is much beneath the surface here and Mr. Hogue's oracle seems to agree.

4th Blood Moon: 28 Sep 2015
According to Rev Hagee and company, this is the last Blood Moon before the start of the Tribulation and the event of the Rapture (Christians taken off of the earth by Jesus Christ at his Second Coming). Mr. Hogue's interpretation (based on astrology and the writings of Nostradamus) is the possibility of nuclear war between the US/NATO and Russia, with Iran being involved as a flashpoint.

I'll let you read the book to get the specific predictions for the Blood Moons, but be aware that they are not in the form of inevitable predictions as is the case with Biblical prophecies expounded on by Christian fundamentalists. That is, rather than "this will happen because God said it would in His Word," we have astrology and the words of seers over the ages to indicate some definite tendencies coming together with certain possible consequences--if we don't do something about them.

That may sound like hedging, but it is, in fact, the actual result of the study of prophetic works (like parts of the Bible and the writings of Nostradamus and other seers). A skilled, honest, prophet (or psychic

Predictions for the Last Blood Moon

sensitive) can examine this material and make definite predictions and/or comment on the likely directions of nations and nature. Warnings and wisdom come from such study.

Where Mr. Hogue expounds on this in *Predictions for the Last Blood Moon* is very interesting. I don't think I've heard him talk about this view of prophecy as being NOT inevitable so much and so well as he does in this book's fourth chapter. It struck a chord with me, especially in his relating this concept to the evangelical proponents of Biblical prophecy (i.e., the Hal Lindsey vein). Because this fundamentalist culture is where I come from, I recognize the reality he is talking about and can only "amen" passages such as:

> *"Inevitability has been embraced by Bible prophecy watchers like John Hagee who shepherd their flock into a state of powerlessness wherein they cannot envision the future beyond being fixed and immutable. I have looked into the same scriptures, and more than this, I have compared one tradition's take on the future with others because belief in destiny's inevitability can only thrive if you limit your imagination or surrender it to self-puffed-up pundits playing holier than thou."*

I also recognize Mr. Hogue's knowledge of the Bible as it relates to prophecy and Christian doctrine. I can appreciate the sympathy he extends to those "born again believers" when he says:

> *"If you find yourself every Sunday sitting in a massive, super-charged, super-churched "pew," deep down hides a girl screaming mindlessly at the Beatles. Know this, that rocking and holy rolling to a shepherd Fuehrer playing religious hysteria's "flock" star is slowly taking your intelligence under the "screaming-at-the-Beatles" spell of mass mindlessness. No true spiritual understanding is possible."*

And that's very true. Been there; done that; got the T-shirt.

Though *Predictions for the Last Blood Moon* is a short book (some 66 pages), it contains much of substance that challenges the "inevitable" view of prophecy and blind-belief systems. In examining the prophetic implications of the recent Blood Moon tetrad, it highlights the trends of current events we should be wary of. For those not satisfied with the dogma of the usual Bible prophecy "scholars," it offers alternative thoughts that can be pursued in Mr. Hogue's other works (several are listed at the book's end, with sample chapters).

And for those spiritually seeking their way through life, this book offers encouragement and suggests a tool for enlightened understanding--wake up and meditate!

Francis and the Last Pope Prophecies of St. Malachy

Author: John Hogue
Publisher: HogueProphecy Publishing
Publication date: 09/26/2015
Pages: 89
ASIN: B015VNYQLE
Type: Nonfiction, Prophecy
Ray's rating: 5 stars

The first version of this review appeared on the www.booklikes.com, www.goodreads.com, and www.amazon.com websites in October of 2015.

RAY-VIEW

WILL Pope Francis be the final pope? Will the years of his pontificate be the years of tribulation that lead to the Apocalypse and God's final judgement of humanity?

Those are the questions addressed by prophecy scholar John Hogue in his book: *Francis and the Last Pope Prophecies of St. Malachy*. This book is a primer on evaluating the St. Malachy Prophecies that count down the popes to the Apocalypse. In it, Mr. Hogue also points out the controversies and contradictions of the Roman Catholic Church, the pageantry and ritual of the pope selection process, and the portents that accompanied that process for the current Pope Francis (formally Cardinal Jorge Bergoglio). He also points out how many of our ideas about Jesus and Christianity (the virgin birth, a bearded Jesus, celibacy for priests, even the resurrection) are the results of the "Romanization" of Christianity. This is interesting material in itself and it provides a context for the St. Malachy material that should help the discerning reader decide whether Pope Francis is indeed the last pope before the End Times kick in.

Mr. Hogue's book examines an old document of "111 mysterious Latin mottoes followed by an apocalyptic coda forecasting the succession of popes to Judgment Day." Legend says it was produced from the ecstatic utterances of St. Malachy (an Irish Prelate) around 1140 when he arrived at Rome at the end of a pilgrimage. Malachy gave his prophecies

Francis and the Last Pope Prophecies

to the pope of that time, Innocent II, who then stored them in the Vatican vaults where they stayed until they were rediscovered in the late 16th century. Mr. Hogue points out that the first 76 mottoes are 100 percent accurate in describing those popes before 1595. He believes these were written after the fact, "sometime after 1557." That makes the remaining 35 mottoes to be actual attempts at foretelling the future, and as such, they are remarkable. Mr. Hogue judges them to have a "success rate" of about 89 percent at identifying future popes (relative to 1557 or so).

St. Malachy's (or whomever's) mottoes are just that--short phrases seldom more than three words in length. For example, #79 reads in English, "A Perverse People" and #83 reads, "Guardian of the Mountains." Each is supposed to identify the specific pope for that point in the succession of popes from St. Peter (although whether #1 actually identifies St. Peter, the disciple of Christ, is not noted). The identification of a given pope is derived from the associated motto by considering 11 prophetic clues. One or more of them should work to explain how the motto uniquely fits the man elected Pope. Mr. Hogue explains this process in chapters Two and Four.

In chapter Two, Mr. Hogue lists the prophetic clues and gives examples of how they work with the mottoes to identify popes. In Chapter Four, he takes each of the 35 genuinely prophetic mottoes, starting with #77 ("A Roman Cross" identifying Clement VIII 1592-1605), and describes how they identify (a hit) or fail to identify (a miss) the associated pope. He goes all the way to #111 ("From the Glory of the Olive" identifying Benedict XVI, 2005-?). The last motto (which would be #112) is actually a paragraph coda that identifies the final pope. These chapters make for a compelling read.

Mr. Hogue's knowledge of prophecy, history, and Latin lend credence to his examination of the mottoes. The many hits and few misses he describes should leave all but the most skeptical of readers with an appreciation for the outstanding nature of the St. Malachy document.

In chapters Five through Eight, Mr. Hogue offers some discussion on the pontificates of the latest popes, Catholic vs non-Catholic ideas about the Apocalypse, some positive thoughts about Pope Francis and whether Nostradamus identified him. In Chapter Nine, he gets to the main question: Is Pope Francis the last pope?

I won't give away Mr. Hogue's answer, but in considering it, you should bear in mind the fluid nature of prophecy and precognition. Seers may be seeing a particular future happening, but these events can change if factors leading up to them change, such as enough desire to make sure they don't happen. From such come prophetic misses, making the accuracy of the St. Malachy prophecies all the more amazing. It would seem that only a few men with destinies to be pope, didn't make it.

So if we're dealing with some real prophecy here, what do we make of it? It seems to me that the preponderance of the world's prophetic literature comes down to a point of unprecedented calamity followed by either human extinction or a turn to a time of enlightened, sustainable living. The importance of the St. Malachy prophecies is that they seem to provide a countdown to this final time. The listing of all popes to the last one, is a pretty definite clock and it is lent much credence just from being so accurate. Hence, the importance of this book that presents that timeline in its historic and prophetic context. It is another validation that we are living at a hugely momentous point in the long human drama.

Francis and the Last Pope Prophecies of St. Malachy is a little book that deals with a big subject, namely, the fate of humanity. For if the seer behind St. Malachy's prophecies has it right, we've reached the end of history: Yeshua will return to set us straight, or we'll pass through the fire that will prompt us to set ourselves straight, or we'll go extinct. Such are the ponderings prompted by prophecies, the events of our time, and whether Pope Francis is the last pope.

The Future

Source: Ray's Journal, www.rayfoy.com, 03-Nov-2013

WHEN I was in high school, a book on Biblical prophecy came out that gained some notoriety and was considered "scary" by my classmates. It was *The Late Great Planet Earth* by Hal Lindsey. In this book, Lindsey interpreted prophetic sections of the Bible according to fundamentalist Christian dogma and in the light of (then) current events (the 1970's). It launched Lindsey on a career in Christian nonfiction writing. Lindsey wrote in a tone that was accessible to young fundamentalist Christians of the time, of which I was one.

I read *The Late Great Planet Earth* many times and adopted its view during that phase of my life when I was of that mindset. Of course, I lived in the deep (US) south where that mindset was predominant. The idea that Biblical prophecy was coming true in our time and that the Rapture was near, was in popular vogue, and I heard many sermons preached on the subject. I was sure that Jesus would return soon, and was glad that I would be on board that last Heavenly chariot out of the fallen Earth before Satan finally trashed everything.

Some years later, I changed my mind about all that. When I read *The Late Great Planet Earth* now, I almost laugh out loud. That's a comment on Mr. Lindsey's writing, however, and not on Biblical prophecy. I still take the Bible seriously, just not literally, or through a dogmatic filter.

I went through a period of agnostic materialism when I didn't consider any "supernatural" subjects as having validity and certainly not any prophecy or fortune-telling. That phase didn't last, though. It succumbed to further readings, research, introspection, and personal experiences. I returned to the idea of extrasensory insight and the paranormal through the work and writings of John Edward, Dannion Brinkley, George Anderson, Whitley Strieber, Shirley MacLaine, John Hogue, and many others. I was then able to seriously consider again the idea of prophecy, and not just the biblical kind.

Now in addition to the works of these writers, there are the works of more conventional, scientific, prophets that I've also read over the

Ray-views

years. These include James Kunstler, Richard Heinberg, Mike Ruppert, Dimitri Orlov, and many others. They base their opinions on the consequences of world events and trends (peak oil, climate change, overpopulation, financial collapse). They tend to agree with the seers, past and present--things don't look so good for humanity right now. There's a really good chance, that we're all hosed.

One reason humans have been so successful in our time on earth is that we are able to look ahead, to visualize the future and so make plans. This, with our intelligence to "figure things out," gave us a huge advantage over animals that were simply big and strong. The price of that capability for outlook is melancholy when a dark future is discerned, or when we look ahead to contemplate our own deaths. Handling this is the wise person's dilemma.

The bleak future described in *The Late Great Planet Earth* was tempered with a "pie in the sky" hope for the afterlife. When you reach the point where you can't take comfort in such a fanciful outcome, what do you do? How do you face a future that indicates no good ending for prevailing momentums?

I don't know. Perhaps you don't "face it" as such. Maybe you live in the eternal "Now," giving and receiving love to enrich your soul and those around you. If enough of us do that, maybe it can build the pressure to trip a switch and answer that last call for fundamental reforms. There's indications it has happened before. Humans have come close to extinction, and pulled through. So I wouldn't write us off for doing it again, though the odds look slimmer this time. There may yet be a faint hope that humanity will break through the ribbon that marks the limit of growth and, after much pain, *live* in the future.

Suggested for Further Reading

Riddle of the Future by Andrew MacKenzie

Book of the Hopi by Frank Waters

Ray-views

The Dystopian Potential

THE BOOKS in this category reflect the potential for a dystopian world to develop at this dark time in humanity's earthly sojourn. It seems that, regardless of people's general distraction, the seldom-spoken consensus is that our industrial civilization is collapsing. Few people believe their children's lives will be better than theirs, and for those that look more deeply, our situation appears even worse.

The "On Prophecy" category contains books that describe prophecies by seers across history that point to a time (our time, apparently) of great problems (tribulation) before some end or great change. The forces that culminate in this tribulation have been working among humans for centuries. They originated at a specific time of great change in human history (see "The Human Problem" category). That change has since rolled over the world leaving a wake of megalomaniac rulers, empires, and totalitarian regimes. We know these forces as Dominator, Taker, Fascist, Austerity, the One Percent, and Neoliberal. They have ruled humanity for some ten thousand years. They prompt opposition, to one degree or other, from the common population—the laborers.

I think that there may be no event in history, since Spartacus' rebellion, where the class war came to blows as openly as in the Spanish Civil War (1936 – 1939). It was widely known at the time who the bad guys were, and they were readily identified as "fascists." They were the corporations, big-business owners, banks, and top managers who manipulated the economy to drain wealth from the workers to the point of pushing them to starvation in the midst of plenty. When a leftist government was finally voted into Spanish office, the expelled conservatives (Nationals, identified as "fascists") attempted a military coup. When that failed, they became "rebels" in a fight to regain their power. Common people rose up to support the government and were themselves supported by volunteers from around the world. The Nationals, were supported by the fascist regimes in Germany and Italy. In the end, the antifascists lost, but the ideology of their struggle echoes to this day. Movies made about that time either ignore the class struggle that was the Spanish Civil War, or pay respectful homage to it (like Casablanca, though indirectly). I suppose the same is true for books and the one that really touched me on this subject was Hemingway's *For Whom the Bell Tolls*.

In the Spanish Civil War, the ruling and working classes fought open battles with armies. That kind of open fighting in the class war is rare, however. Normally it is suppressed and operates quietly within the system, and sometimes, the elites have to deal with opposition from one of "their own." I believe that was the case with US President John Kennedy and this can be seen in a careful reading of Robert Dallek's *An Unfinished Life: John F. Kennedy, 1917-1963*.

Mr. Dallek's biography of JFK shows a man who grew up in a bubble of privilege to the point that he didn't realize the extent of the ruling class' malevolent control until he was well into his presidency. At first he went along with the agenda, ignoring the civil rights movement, opposing the spread of communism, and pursuing the goals of overthrowing Fidel Castro and ramping up a war in Vietnam. At some point, though, conscience caught up with him and he reached a line he could not cross. I suspect that Franklin Roosevelt, and even Abraham Lincoln, reached a similar point.

Then President Kennedy started trying to do the right thing. He sent in federal marshals to see that James Meredith was enrolled at the University of Mississippi, he withheld US military support of the Bay of Pigs invasion, and he stopped sending "advisors" to Vietnam with the intention of pulling out the ones already there. Even during the Cuban Missile Crisis, he worked feverishly with Soviet First Secretary Nikita Khrushchev to oppose the hawkish generals on both sides and so avoid nuclear war. Contrast this with more recent presidents who talked peace while campaigning and then ramped up wars when in office.

Many Kennedy scholars think that his decision to stop the buildup to war in Vietnam was his undoing with the elites, and made his assassination inevitable. That may indeed have been his final straw on top of a lot of initiatives the elites didn't like. A review of history shows that Lyndon Johnson, Kennedy's successor, had no reservations about promoting war and pursuing the ruling class agenda. All this can be seen in Mr. Dallek's book (if indirectly), although he wrote it with a far more conventional viewpoint.

Because we live in a dominator world culture (see *The Chalice & The Blade* in the "The Human Problem" category), the seeds for a dystopian society are always present. Two of the books Ray-viewed in this category are there because I think they expose the significant seed of racism. Race is an easy tool for dividing a population, especially when it is primed with a history of one race being enslaved by another. Old hatreds linger. The

The Dystopian Potential

"race card" has been played to perfection by the US oligarchy and that's why *To Kill a Mockingbird* is so poignant in its portrayal of the day-to-day racism in the US south. Harper Lee shows us that beneath the veneer of white and black people getting along, the division is there, ready to be split, violently.

This "dividing rod" of racial mistrust is also spotlighted in James Meredith's memoir, *A Mission from God*. The attitudes of hatred he describes in his breaking of the color barrier to enroll at the University of Mississippi in the early 1960s, are those counted on by the oligarchs to keep the common people divided. Otherwise, if we were brought together, say by some issue like opposing the Vietnam War, we might unite against those at the top who profit from our misery (or at least, from our delusions).

With such a history that is defined by class warfare, what do we come up with when we try to project that history into the future? Certainly, there are classic works that do just that: *1984* and *Brave New World* come to mind. These describe dystopian futures that are still valid to consider. For this category, however, I chose more recent books.

There are varying degrees of realism in the books and movies that depict dystopian futures. One version is epic and uses the "Hero's Journey" theme. In these stories, people are oppressed by an evil regime that is opposed by rebels who are united and led to victory by a hero, who is usually a youth chosen by higher powers for this task. *Star Wars* is a prime example. *Eragon* is another (books and the movie). Even many video games follow this template. There are scads of novels put out every day that use this theme. They're good when they are done well, but they are usually shallow and don't approach the introspective depths of say, *1984* or *For Whom the Bell Tolls*.

One notable exception is Suzanne Collins' *Hunger Games* books. These are dystopian future, action stories, but with such a solid underpinning of class warfare that they could serve as an introduction to the concept for young people. And Ms Collins is hardly subtle with her books' metaphors. The oligarchs rule from a city called, "Capitol" (capital) from whence they suck up all the wealth produced by the labor of the 12 districts. The people in the districts are left with just enough to survive and are brutally punished if they seek to better their lots on their own. A police force of "peace keepers" keep them in line. These books are brilliant for their depiction of rulers pretending benevolence and common people (laborers) accepting it all out of hopelessness. There's even a Middle Class that is as clueless as it is decadent. While I don't think *Hunger*

Ray-views

Games is accurate in its view of our future, I think it is quite accurate in describing our present.

James Kunstler's *The Witch of Hebron* is a deliberate attempt to describe our likely future. It's actually the second book in a series that began with *World Made by Hand*. In these books, Mr. Kunstler shows our future as being collapsed to a lower, roughly 19th century, level. People live very locally with practically no awareness of the world outside their town and immediate countryside. They live off the remains of our technology with little access to fossil fuels. They grow their own food and get around on foot and horseback. There is lawlessness and many who practice banditry, but it's not an over-the-top, *Mad Max* type of lawlessness. In the spite of bandits and their struggles to survive, people build communities with local rules and local authorities. They strive to retain the best of what was lost.

I like Mr. Kunstler's books and I think they are realistic up to a point. I just think collapse won't be so simple as losing access to cheap gasoline and manufacturing. I think it will be greatly complicated by ecological disaster from geoengineering and climate change that will make agriculture and human-compatible environments problematic. Still, these books offer much to consider in contemplating collapse.

A much darker view of our future is offered in Cormac McCarthy's *The Road*. It is set in a world that has fallen from apocalyptic circumstances (war, pestilence, etc) rather than the consequences of an "endless growth" paradigm. I suspect, though, that the fall can be just as far from either cause. Mr. McCarthy goes further than Mr. Kunstler, however, in describing the depths of the fallen world. He notes that the earth will no longer grow food (Gaia's rebellion or sickness?) and the weather is constantly gray, with a gray ash covering everything. The only food to be found is whatever has survived. Some people turn to cannibalism. This state of affairs offers the survivors no hope beyond being the "last standing." That's bleak, but it provides an exploration of finding a reason to live when all is hopeless. The protagonist in *The Road* finds his reason in caring for his son, echoing Viktor Frankl's experiences with surviving hopelessness (see *Man's Search for Meaning* in the "Inspiration" category).

By and large, I think the only fiction genre that portrays a hopeful future for humanity is hard science fiction. *Star Trek* is one example (*2001: A Space Odyssey* is another) and I think that comes from a faith in (and love of) technology. That faith is as much a backlash against the doom of reality as anything, and I believe that was the case in the 1960s when the *Star Trek* TV series came out. It's actually a very hopeful and inspiring

The Dystopian Potential

series that spited the Cold War, but I think it is fantasy in the face of the way the world is unwinding.

Indeed, most fiction, when it projects the future, shows it as fallen and dark (as in David Mitchell's brilliant *Cloud Atlas;* see the "Beyond the Usual" category). I think this is a reflection of the general attitude, which is largely an unconscious one since most people don't seem to consider the future any more than they consider the sky over their heads. While it seems that, of the works cited here, *The Road* may best depict our future, we must remember that there is a thread in the predictions of seers through history of a positive future for humanity after a period of tribulation. This may be just us telling ourselves that we can make it through, but we need that positive self-talk. After all, as we learned from the books in the "On Prophecy" section, predictions are of possibilities that, no matter how dire, can be changed.

Personally, I think it would be a tremendous salvation for humanity to change it's fate from *The Road* to *World Made by Hand.*

For Whom the Bell Tolls

Author: Ernest Hemingway
Publisher: Scribner
Publication date: 2003 (first published 1940)
Pages: 471
ISBN-13: 9780684803357
Type: Fiction, War, Class Struggle
Ray's rating: 4 stars
Characters: Maria, Pilar, Robert Jordan, Pablo, Anselmo

The first version of this review appeared on the www.goodreads.com and www.booklikes.com websites in April of 2014.

RAY-VIEW

FOR WHOM THE BELL TOLLS is Ernest Hemingway's story of an American volunteer helping the Spanish peasant militias fight the fascist "rebels" in the Spanish Civil War. It is a compelling and educational tale that is a picture of a particular time coupled with keen insight into one lucid moment of class warfare. I loved this book and highly recommend it as a literary classic and as an insight into an important time in human history.

The endnotes in the edition of *For Whom the Bell Tolls* that I read, say that Ernest Hemingway "reported on the Spanish Civil War." He must have reported it very well because his novel has all the gritty feel of action spiced with the politics and personalities of the partisan and fascist fighters. Indeed, the term, "Spanish Civil War" is never used in the book and while it isn't necessary to realize that this is the war being fought to appreciate Hemingway's story, it helps to have some historical knowledge of it.

The story is mostly told from the viewpoint of its primary protagonist, Robert Jordan. Jordan is an American teacher of Spanish who has joined the fight against fascism in Spain, circa 1937. He has become an expert in using explosives and is on a mission to support an attack of Russian units against the fascists (or "Nationals") by blowing up a bridge. He enlists the aid of a guerrilla band of Spaniards in the mountains. This band is lead by Pablo, who has apparently lost his courage since the early days of the war when he was ruthless against the fascists. Pablo's woman, Pelar, is with them. She is wise and an effective

For Whom the Bell Tolls

storyteller who gives Jordan a vivid picture of those early days when Pablo was at his best. Then there's Maria, a fugitive from the fascists who was rescued by Pablo's group. Love quickly blossoms between Jordan and Maria.

The telling of Jordan's story occurs over about four days. In the telling, Hemingway relates attitudes and beliefs not often portrayed in Hollywood war movies. Take Robert Jordan's reason for joining the fight. Like most of those who volunteered to defend the progressive government against the fascists (who were comprised of the Spanish military, Spanish conservative oligarchs, and German and Italian military units), Jordan is idealistic and fighting for the common man's freedom against oppression. At one point, in a kind of soliloquy, he says:

> *You learned the dry-mouthed, fear-purged, purging ecstasy of battle and you fought...for all the poor in the world, against all tyranny, for all the things that you believed and for the new world...I love liberty and dignity and the rights of all men to work and not be hungry.*

Fascists prefer that people stay hungry, fearful, and not worried about dignity so they'll be a compliant workforce that will work for next to nothing. Hollywood never gives us the corporate foundation of fascism, but it was well understood in the 1930s and Hemingway certainly understood it in this book.

Hollywood tells us that the 20th century fascists (especially the Nazis) were simply a power-hungry evil. They were that, but they were also good businessmen. Spain was a country of huge income inequality, where the vast majority were desperately poor peasants who worked the fields of agricultural estates. The rich estate owners grew richer off the labor of the peasants who worked for a bare subsistence. The peasants were aware of their oppression, and of who their oppressors were.

When the war erupted, the peasants formed militias and many took their revenge. Hemingway describes one such vengeful episode through the eyes of Pelar as she tells Robert Jordan how Pablo handled a set of executions. In a small village (possibly his home village) Pablo had the local fascists run off a cliff to be dashed onto the jagged rocks below. Those so executed are described as landowners, merchants, traders, insurance agents, and bankers. That list might be surprising to Americans brought up on movies where fascists are Nazis in the German army or bureaucrats in the German government. The association with businessmen and corporations is never made.

Ray-views

But Hemingway's characters are not black-and-white stereotypes. He deals with the gray areas of political associations and how basic human drives and fears touch everyone, especially under the pressures of war. And so the fascists driven to their deaths by Pablo first seek absolution from a priest. Their defiance breaks down into fear. They part in sorrow from loved ones who mourn their loss of parents and spouses without political considerations. Indeed, we get the feeling that the executions are too harsh a punishment in at least some cases. For instance, Pelar notes that:

Don Guillermo was a fascist but otherwise there was nothing against him.

But Don Guillermo was executed anyway.

The crowd of peasants facilitating the deaths, are reluctant to do so at first. They are not killers by nature, even when confronted with those who oppressed them. But they can be led, and as a few get into the "sport," the crowd follows their lead until it becomes a jeering mob, delighting in the killings and absolving themselves by it being a group effort.

Hemingway makes people reconciling themselves to killing and to facing death a major theme. The crowd's reluctance to kill in Pelar's story is mirrored at a personal level by nearly every major character. Most kill because they are in a war and have to, but with varying degrees of reluctance and ways of excusing themselves. Even Pablo, who is described as heartless in ordering the fascist executions, is later seen to have lost his nerve and is doubtful of being able to kill again. Robert Jordan, who is in many ways a technician and approaches killing as a technical necessity, cannot bring himself to kill Pablo even when the consensus is that he should.

Such nuances of characters facing hard decisions and coping with war make the story gripping as the action progresses towards the blowing of the bridge. In the midst of it all is the love story between Robert Jordan and Maria. Their relationship is often cited as a notable literary romance, but I saw it as mostly a device to give Jordan something to live for. His love relationship with Maria is probably true to the time, but it struck me as a bit condescending towards Maria. She has her strengths, but she is too deferential to Jordan and he treats her as a child. He calls her his "rabbit" which I couldn't really relate to, and their future plans are actually *his* future plans (though he comes to show signs of a growing appreciation of her). Still, their love story is a legitimate plot device and it serves its purpose.

For Whom the Bell Tolls

For Whom The Bell Tolls is like an eyewitness account of the Spanish Civil War, but the account goes beyond a relating of events and into how the participants related to those events. The internal struggles of the characters feed into and are fed by the violence around them. How they cope is instructional for us in considering what we would do in a similar situation. Sometimes such instruction is best done in fiction, especially when it's infused with a reality witnessed by the author.

Hemingway entitled this novel from a passage in John Donne's *Meditations*, and prefaces it with that "never send to know for whom the bell tolls" quote. Donne's point is that "we're all in this together" and so we all ultimately go down together whether circumstances make it appear that way or not. I think that is Mr. Hemingway's point as well, and is why he gives names and some backstory for even the most secondary of minor characters before they are killed. He wants us to see that it is human beings who are losing their lives.

John Donne said there is no need to ask for whom the funeral bell is ringing, because we should know. Likewise, there was no need for the fascist commander who beat Sordo's unit to take heads to identify the fallen. They are all of us.

An Unfinished Life: John F. Kennedy, 1917-1963

Author: Robert Dallek, Cynthia Harrod-Eagles
Publisher: Little, Brown & Company
Publication date: 4/7/2004
Pages: 848
ISBN-13: 9780316907927
Type: Nonfiction, Political, Biography
Ray's rating: 3 stars

The first version of this review appeared on the www.goodreads.com website in July of 2012.

RAY-VIEW

AN UNFINISHED LIFE: JOHN F. KENNEDY, 1917-1963 is Robert Dallek's best-selling biography of the United States' 35th president. The book has garnered much critical acclaim and rightly so. Dallek does an admirable job of showing the character of JFK behind his public image and the historical record. I expect most readers will finish this book with an understanding of Kennedy as a genuinely good, though flawed, person who honestly sought to do his duty for the good of the country as President of the United States. But what I see implicit in the narrative is a man engaged with forces he could not control and that finally killed him.

Those forces are the dark, behind-the-scenes, controlling financial, political, hereditarily powerful, elites that exercised much control of the US government in Kennedy's day, and complete control of it now (see Daniel Estulin's *The Shadow Masters*). In Dwight Eisenhower's parlance, they're the Military-Industrial Complex. In Occupy Wall Street parlance, they're the One Percent. They can be seen at work in Dallek's book just from the recitation of historical events, but that Dallek doesn't identify them as a controlling force is, to me, his book's great failing and the reason for my three star rating.

To be sure, the book is about John F Kennedy and it relates the narrative of his life with great detail and engaging prose. We see his development from privileged youth to assuming the role of the "next-in-line son" upon the death of his older brother, his return from war as a

An Unfinished Life

wizened veteran, his political successes abetted by family money, and his struggling as president to find the right way. And he accomplished all this with two glaring flaws--poor health and a sex addiction (though the two would seem to be mutually exclusive).

Kennedy's health problems were such that he went through periods on crutches and debilitated with gastric-based pain. Even so, he pushed himself to engage in athletics (because fitness and being physically active were family expectations) and used his father's political influence to get himself a combat assignment in the Navy during World War II. In fact, one of this book's great revelations (maybe the biggest one) is just how bad JFK's health was throughout his life. But Kennedy kept his condition mostly secret so it wouldn't be used against him in politics or deny him his desired military service. Much of what he accomplished in his life was done in the spite of physical ailments and sheer pain.

Dallek also made much of Kennedy's womanizing, as have others, though "womanizing" may be too polite a term for sex parties with prostitutes and seducing young interns. Even JFK seemed to acknowledge it as a compulsion that he didn't understand. Still, this is not such a revelation about Kennedy, or even about other politicians in high office (Dallek says Lyndon Johnson had a room in the White House dedicated for such activities), but it does lend support to my belief that politicians are bought with sex as much as with campaign contributions.

Beyond these personal aspects of JFK's career, are the better known experiences that Dallek describes in detail bolstered with much research and a thorough bibliography--the fiasco of the Bay of Pigs (cementing JFK's distrust of the CIA and the military), civil rights support (like using the army to assist James Meredith's enrollment at Ole Miss), the Cuban missile crisis, and the US nascent involvement in Vietnam (his final opposition to which was, I believe, his undoing). All are described with interesting detail and intimations of Kennedy's personal take on each, pulled from his own writings or remembrances by people that were there.

So *An Unfinished Life* is a very enlightening tome about John F Kennedy as a man and a president. Historical events are described in detail, engaging the reader with JFK's viewpoint. But Dallek's angle on JFK and his times is very much "traditional" and worse, uncritical, of the political process and the greater perspective of elite greed and corruption that oppresses the current times. As such, it is difficult to read about politicians motivated by the "communist threat" when hindsight holds the United States governments equally responsible for the cold war's threat to world life and peace.

Ray-views

For example, there are numerous passages like this one from Chapter 5 that talks about Kennedy's beginning term as a Senator:

> ...*mounting national concern about the communist threat. With numerous labor walkouts over insufficient wage hikes...and growing fears of communist subversions and expansion...*

This passage is saying that the fear of communism gave the Republicans the Senate and House majorities in 1947. It is uncritical. What were these fears based on? Was communism really a threat to the United States or was the "threat" a cover for competition between totalitarian-imperialist regimes? Was the fear of communism created and egged on by the US elite for political advantage?

Such questions were considered traitorous 30 years ago, but today, surely we have a wider perspective to judge such things with more skepticism and less delusion.

Dallek describes Kennedy's aversion to making US military commitments to protecting the regime of South Vietnam from takeover by North Vietnam, but he does not question the source nor motive of the pressure to make that commitment. He seems to accept the notion of stopping communist aggression, with no mention of the "military-industrial complex" for whom unending war is a source of tremendous profits. When JFK opposed escalating the US involvement in Vietnam, many believe it sealed his doom. He was assassinated and his vice president, who in all else proceeded with Kennedy's agenda, increased the country's involvement in that conflict until it destroyed his presidency along with the fighting capability of the US army, and left a permanent scar on the national conscience (of the common people, not our rulers).

An Unfinished Life is a valuable book, but it should be read with the understanding that it tells John F Kennedy's story from a standpoint that believes in American exceptionalism and the purity of purpose of its elected officials. It believes in the "American Camelot."

Mr. Dallek tells a good story and he brings JFK and his times to life, but I believe the greater story lies between his lines.

To Kill a Mockingbird

Author: Harper Lee
Publisher: Harper Collins
Publication date: 07/08/2014
Pages: 385
ASIN: B00K0OI42W
Type: Fiction, Political, Crime
Ray's rating: 5 stars
Characters: Jean Louise (Scout) Finch, Jeremy (Jem) Finch, Atticus Finch, Tom Robinson (defendant), Dill, Arthur (Boo) Radley

The first version of this review appeared on the www.goodreads.com and www.booklikes.com websites in July of 2015.

RAY-VIEW

    TO KILL A MOCKINGBIRD is the Pulitzer prize winning novel by Nelle Harper Lee published in 1961. Having finally read it, I see why it is a classic. It is sophisticated and nuanced in theme and in the telling, despite its down-home, small town setting. On the whole, I would say it is what *The Andy Griffith Show* would have been had it honestly portrayed the subject of racism in Mayberry--and if Sheriff Taylor had questioned the legal system, and if Opie had precociously questioned Sheriff Taylor, and if Aunt Bea had been black.
    The story is set in the small town of Maycomb, Alabama in 1935. It is told completely from the point-of-view of eight year-old, Jean Louise Finch (also known as "Scout") who is the daughter of fifty-year old widower and lawyer, Atticus Finch. The first half of the book is pretty much like episodic TV, with events happening to Scout, her brother Jem, and their friends against the Mayberry-like setting. But Mayberry was never like Maycomb in the open racism of its citizens. In the first half of the book, this racism is very well established by Ms Lee through liberal use of the "N-word."

...if anybody sees a white n----r around, that's the one..and next time he won't aim high, be it dog, n----r, or--

...but now he's turned out to be a n----r-lover we'll never be able to walk the streets of Maycomb again.

Ray-views

...but around here once you have a drop of Negro blood, that makes you all black.

And so forth. The common hatred of black people in Maycomb and the assumed attitude that black people are inferior to whites is familiar to me, having grown up in the US deep south in the 1960s. I can attest that the picture Ms Lee paints is realistic for that time.

It is in this setting that the story's drama unfolds when a young black man, Tom Robinson, is accused of raping a white woman. Atticus Finch is assigned by the judge to defend Robinson. Atticus is progressively-minded in contrast to those around him and he is very aware of that fact. He knows that taking the case and actually trying to defend Robinson will bring problems for himself and for his children. Wanting to set the right moral example for his kids, Atticus does defend Robinson to the best of his ability, and the problems he expected do arise.

Fans of *To Kill a Mockingbird* are drawn to the engaging characters in it, especially the kids, Scout and Jem. Ms Lee shows them moving through their world, dealing with school and adults, having school-yard fights, being obsessed with their reclusive neighbor, fearing "haints" and mad dogs. This is the "episodic" part but it includes some brilliant observations on southern, small town life that underscores the uglier racism.

For example, the inadequacy of the education system that actually retards the development of precocious children. Scout's view of her first years in elementary school is:

...as I inched sluggishly along the treadmill of the Maycomb County school system, I could not help receiving the impression that I was being cheated out of something.

And the southern obsession with fundamentalist Protestant religion that tolerates only conformity (mirroring the intolerance for blacks) prompts Scout to make an observation on some church people's condemnation of a neighbor for being more concerned with caring for her garden than for Bible study:

My confidence in pulpit Gospel lessened at the vision of Miss Maudie stewing forever in various Protestant hells.

But the central conflict in the story is the Robinson trial and its anticlimax. In that telling, Ms Lee expresses an interesting lack of confidence in the impartial rule-of-law. In Atticus' summation to the jury,

To Kill a Mockingbird

he extolls, eloquently, the virtue of a court system as the only place in society where men are truly equal:

...in this country our courts are the great levelers, and in our courts all men are created equal.

But he follows with a qualification:

A court is only as sound as its jury, and a jury is only is only as sound as the men who make it up.

We see later that Atticus has no confidence that the jury will do the right thing, because of the attitudes of the men who make it up. And thus is the book's indictment of US society. It's also, I think, what made it a Pulitzer winner.

But even more interesting to me, was the story's attitude towards the law in the anticlimax. I don't do spoilers, so I'll just say that this lack of confidence in the court system for finding justice is extended when some characters circumvent it to protect an innocent. There is a certain amount of judgementalness in this that might seem hypocritical, and indeed, the characters (especially Atticus) wrestle with it. But they make their choices and deciding the moral rightness of their actions is, I think, an exercise left to the reader.

To Kill a Mockingbird is a classic piece of literature greatly beloved by readers for good reason. It is beautifully written with an intimate feel for its characters and appreciation for the nuances of life, especially where big issues are concerned.

This book is Mayberry with a sharp edge.

A Mission from God: A Memoir and Challenge for America

Author: James Meredith (with William Doyle)
Publisher: Atria Books
Publication date: 8/7/2012
Pages: 288
ISBN-13: 9781451674729
Type: Nonfiction, Political, History
Ray's rating: 4 stars
Characters:

The first version of this review appeared on the www.goodreads.com website in April of 2013.

RAY-VIEW

A MISSION FROM GOD: A MEMOIR AND CHALLENGE FOR AMERICA by James Meredith is an important record of a particular time in American history. Mr. Meredith's recounting of his experiences in the turmoil of the Civil Rights movement in the 1960s is an apt example to us of the dynamics of resisting an oppressive system. That system is shown in Mr. Meredith's book as the institutionalized notion of the superiority of the Caucasian race in the US state of Mississippi. It was the evil progeny of the feudal plantation system of the old south that was built on the foundation of chattel slavery. After the south's loss in the Civil War, the system evolved into one of enforced societal segregation between whites and blacks, with laws that nullified Federal laws and resulted in continued oppression of the former slaves.

The southern culture could not stand the idea of black people (actually, all nonwhite people) being equal with whites in intellect, political rights, and humanity. Mr. Meredith shines a light on this attitude, describing its prevalence among Mississippi leaders and white citizens as well as its violent edge. This system then, this belief in racial superiority is the enemy that Mr. Meredith opposes with acts that challenged its legitimacy and provoked its anger.

James Meredith is best known for two events: being the first black American to enroll in and earn a degree from the University of Mississippi (Ole Miss), and for being shot. His book opens with a recounting of the latter, which serves as a frame for the Ole Miss events.

A Mission from God

In June of 1966, some three years after he graduated from Ole Miss, Mr. Meredith began a one-person march (though others joined him) from Memphis to Jackson with the intent of promoting his call for black people in Mississippi to register to vote. This was big because black people were generally afraid to register and only did so in the face of laws (poll tax, literacy tests, etc) that would prevent them from voting in any case. Mr. Meredith describes the start of his march down highway 51 to strike another blow at the beast of white supremacy. Just outside of the little town of Hernando, the beast took human form as a poor white from the sticks acting on the local tenet of "I'd just as soon kill a n----r as look at him," and Mr. Meredith was shot-gunned in cold blood and left for dead.

From there, Mr. Meredith switches to an account of his background and thoughts on the times, and then begins his narrative about attending Ole Miss (which was the bigger event though no less life-threatening). In this section, he gets into his reputation as a civil rights rebel--contributing to the movement but never being a part of it. He makes no bones about his personal pride and near messiah complex. He was (and is) opinionated and driven to confuse, confound, and confront. This comes through in his writing and nearly put me off at a couple of points. I'm suspicious of people that proudly proclaim themselves as mavericks and declare that they confound others. It's an implication of superiority that is usually unfounded. But I hung with him and decided that, on balance, he comes off as a sympathetic character that genuinely cares about others. Indeed, his attitude of self-confidence and spiritual mission was probably the lightning rod that made him the exemplary focus of the civil rights struggle at the time.

Mr. Meredith describes the University of Mississippi as a bastion of white supremacy. Though a public university, it provided the formal higher-education for most of the state's leaders and maintained an aristocratic ambiance that was exclusive of poor whites as well as minorities. Today it is racially integrated, but there is still an air of that exclusiveness. When Mr. Meredith sought to enroll there, he was met with a violent racial bias that led to riots. He describes his repeated attempts to enroll as the last battle of the Civil War and accounts indicate that he's pretty much correct in that assessment. The inertia against him built to the point that mobs violently opposed the federal marshals (and later the soldiers of the army and national guard) that escorted him at enrollment and in just attending his classes. In all the chaos, shots were fired and people were killed.

The account of his enrollment and time at Ole Miss constitutes the main part of the book. Mr. Meredith describes in graphic detail the anger and torments visited on him throughout his time there. I suspect that many readers, especially younger ones not from the south, will find this narrative hard to believe. After all, you can walk around the Ole Miss campus today, or peruse its website, and see that it's thoroughly integrated and looks like any other university campus. But it was very different in the early 1960s. I was a child then and only vaguely aware of the events centering on James Meredith, but I can affirm the attitudes he describes and the sheer hatred towards black people among working and middle class whites. A quick study of history will affirm his account of the "battle" that erupted from his Ole Miss enrollment. Robert Dallek gives a similar description of it in his book about John Kennedy (*An Unfinished Life*).

In describing his abuse by the white students at Ole Miss, Mr. Meredith is graphic, quoting their constant use of derogatory terms, insults and harassments. But his account is without any reciprocal hatred of them as people. I expect time has tempered his emotions but he does say, regarding his harassers, that "They were programmed to act the way they did." Having grown up in Mississippi, I would concur.

Mr. Meredith graduated from Ole Miss in August of 1963. His ordeal there was barely a year in length (most of his credits to graduate were transferred from other colleges). His military escort around the campus had shrunk and the expressions of hatred had subsided, mostly from familiarity. He graduated and left, with the implied "good riddance" from staff and students, but he opened a door that others entered.

At this point, Mr. Meredith returns to his ordeal on the road outside of Hernando. Lying on the ground, shot, a picture is taken of him by a reporter and it becomes iconic. The initial news of his death, was corrected after an hour or so and he was taken to a hospital. His march to Jackson was completed by Martin Luther King and other civil rights leaders. Mr. Meredith himself recovered enough to complete the march amid a crowd that he didn't intend.

Here, he talks about his differences with the civil rights leaders of the day, especially with regards to strict adherence to nonviolence as their primary tactic. Mr. Meredith believed that force was the only way to overcome the violence that the white supremacist establishment used with impunity. He is referring in this to the use of force by the federal government to make state governments comply with the law. This is what worked for him and his impression of the effectiveness of that force, and his gratitude for it, thoroughly infuse this book.

A Mission from God concludes with Mr. Meredith's reflection on growing old, finding meaning in his life, and retaining his sense of mission in his final years. To me, this is the books most poignant part. He went

A Mission from God

to Japan to complete work on the book. It was a return for him. He had spent three years there when in the Air Force and was touched by the people's lack of prejudice towards him. It was a place he felt acceptance as a human being and it became the symbol for him of that place of equality that Martin Luther King dreamed of beyond the mountain. As an old man, Mr. Meredith climbed Mount Takao and found his renewed inspiration there amidst nature. He heard the voice of God again, renewing his sense of mission.

I think I've finally figured out what old men are supposed to do. They are supposed to finish things they haven't finished, and teach things they have learned to young people. Everybody talks about Moses leading children out of Egypt, but people forget how many times he tried before he succeeded. He only succeeded as an old man.

That new mission is the challenge part of his book. He asks the reader to commit to helping children in public schools, especially disadvantaged children. He believes such an outpouring of love directed at the support of the nation's children, would transform America into the good place it is supposed to be, and that fulfills its potential as a moral leader in the world.

I expect it would indeed.

The Hunger Games

Author: Suzanne Collins
Publisher: Scholastic, Inc.
Publication date: 7/1/2010
Pages: 384
ISBN-13: 9780439023528
Type: Fiction, Science Fiction & Fantasy, Dystopian
Ray's rating: 4 stars
Characters: Katniss Everdeen, Peeta Mellark, Gale Hawthorne, Haymitch Abernathy, Caesar Flickerman, Effie Trinket

The first version of this review appeared on the www.goodreads.com website in December of 2013.

RAY-VIEW

THE HUNGER GAMES is a speculative novel set in our dystopian future that is a mirror and scathing commentary on our dystopian present. Its socialist theme of brutally exploited workers is spot-on for our time and will resonate with open-minded readers of the "ninety-nine percent." But it's also a well-told, exciting tale of imagination that author Suzanne Collins melds agreeably with its weighty theme. Doing so while writing at a Young Adult level is a testament to Ms Collins' skill, though I have some technical criticisms in that area that cause me to withhold a fifth star from my rating.

Ms Collin' story tightly follows the point-of-view of Katniss Everdeen, a teenager living in our future where the US has become a nation called, "Panem," that is divided into 12 districts ruled from the capitol city simply called, "Capitol" (located somewhere in the Rocky Mountains). Capitol rules brutally and at one point the districts rebelled. Capitol's victory in that war resulted in the establishment of the annual "Hunger Games" as a punishment of the districts. Every year, each district is required to send one boy and one girl, referred to as "tributes," between the ages of 12 and 18, to a designated expanse of ground where they must fight to the death. The winner is simply the single surviving tribute.

The games are Panem's annual humiliation of the districts and a reminder to them of their place in the scheme of things. They exist only to supply the material needs for Capitol (crops, coal, etc) with each district

The Hunger Games

specializing in some basic item. This is a picture of globalization, where the developed West conquers and exploits the "third world" to supply its material needs (oil, minerals, cheap labor, etc). As in the real world, the producers don't benefit from what they produce, it's all shipped off to market and the workers are left hungry and in want. They are not allowed to feed themselves; food is to be bought from Capitol with earnings from their life-consuming labor. If people in the districts feed themselves by hunting, trading in the black market, or otherwise providing for their survival, they are breaking the law. That's what Katniss does in hunting in the forbidden forest with her friend, Gale, and then taking advantage of the corrupt officials by selling them game (this kind of gray-area subtlety is what gives the book its power).

Tributes for the Hunger Games are chosen by a lottery in an event called, "the Reaping." It is done separately for the boys and girls from names entered for those within the eligible ages. Names can be entered multiple times in exchange for extra allocations of grain and oil. Though Katniss has her name in multiple times, the bad luck of the draw falls on her little sister, Prim. As the frightened Prim makes her way to the stage to stand as this year's "winner" for the girls, Katniss volunteers to take her place, which the rules allow. From there, Katniss, and the boy tribute, Peeta Mellark, are swept away by train to the Capitol where they are groomed to participate in the preliminary hoopla before the fight-to-the-death spectacle.

Part of the humiliation visited on the districts by the Hunger Games is the way Capitol treats them as an entertainment and something akin to an athletic competition. Athletic skill, however, is in no way a qualification--twelve year old girls are thrown in the arena with 18 year old young men who have trained all their lives to win the games (these are known as "careers"). Much pomp and ceremony surrounds the tributes and the lead-up to the games is highly publicized. The tributes are interviewed on TV and treated as celebrities, with no mention of their impending deaths, simply the prospect of winning or losing. This death denial on the part of the Capitol public fits with their depiction as self-absorbed, artificial, and materialistic.

Once the book gets into the actual games, the action is fast and gritty as we watch Katniss trying to survive, evading the careers, making "alliances," playing to the audience for support (cameras are hidden everywhere in the "natural environment" of the arena and the whole thing is televised), and working out her uncertain relationship with her fellow District 12 tribute, Peeta. It all leads to a satisfying conclusion that sets up the storyline to continue in the next book (*Catching Fire*).

Ray-views

What impresses me most about *The Hunger Games* is its subtle depiction of the overwhelming power of Capitol. There are no scenes of pitched battles with the oppressed populace (in this book) or of people just talking about how bad Capitol is. Often, dystopian stories will use such scenes to show the badness of the rulers, but they are usually too contrived to be believable. Ms Collins shows Capitol's malevolent power in the sheer unwinding of the games according to the yearly program. The people just go along with it because they have no choice, and so their sons and daughters are taken from them for slaughter. The tears of the tributes are a stark contrast to the jubilations of the Capitol spectators who, in shallow delusion, view the games as just games. Over it all, the rulers of Capitol are in control, working out their program to keep the districts under submission. All through the story, you get the feeling of irresistible power and inevitable control by the rulers (represented by President Snow). It makes the instances of resistance by Katniss feel even more heroic, if futile.

As I said, *The Hunger Games* is written as a Young Adult novel and the language is at that level. At times it seems a bit too YA where I think it would only have helped to elevate it some. The narrative is also written in the present tense ("I am doing this" instead of "I did that") which I found annoying at times. I think a normal past tense would have worked better. Also, the point-of-view never leaves Katniss and so Ms Collins misses some opportunities to round out her story with perspectives that beg to grow from her otherwise excellent storyline. The movie acts on this and so provides a greater spotlight on the Capitol citizens' deluded callousness (especially in the character of the "talk show" host, Caesar Flickerman who is so wonderfully brought to life by actor Stanley Tucci), and on the cruel duplicity of Panem's rulers as represented by President Snow (brilliantly played with a subtle ominousness by Donald Sutherland).

I think the three books in *The Hunger Games* series will constitute a dystopian classic in the vein of *1984* and *Brave New World*. As such, I am much surprised that it was even made into a movie (I'm less surprised that the movie has been a huge success, since it is faithful to the book). I guess the elites feel a fiction set in the future can be easily dismissed in the present. I would advise you not to dismiss *The Hunger Games*, however. It's an exciting and thoughtful story, and a picture of our times.

Catching Fire

Author: Suzanne Collins
Publisher: Scholastic, Inc.
Publication date: 6/4/2013
Pages: 400
ISBN-13: 9780545586177
Type: Fiction, Science Fiction & Fantasy, Dystopian
Ray's rating: 4 stars
Characters: Katniss Everdeen, Peeta Mellark, Gale Hawthorne, Haymitch Abernathy, Caesar Flickerman, Effie Trinket

The first version of this review appeared on the www.goodreads.com and www.booklikes.com websites in December of 2013.

RAY-VIEW

CATCHING FIRE is the second novel in Suzanne Collins' trilogy about our dystopian future. It is a fine bridge between the first and third novels (*The Hunger Games* and *Mockingjay*) taking the story's telling of action against oppression from passive resistance to open rebellion.

The setting for all the novels is the future North America that has become the nation of Panem, comprised of twelve districts brutally ruled by a central capitol city ("Capitol"). In return for their bare survival, the districts work to provide the material needs of Capitol. Some skirt the law and provide for themselves by hunting and black market trading. Among these are Katniss Everdeen, a seventeen year old girl struggling to take care of her mother and little sister after the death of her father. In *The Hunger Games*, we saw her participate in the annual fight-to-the-death of young people (called "tributes," aged 12 to 18) drawn from the twelve districts, when she volunteered to replace her young sister. This fight, (a "game" to the deluded and hedonistic citizens of Capitol) is done every year as punishment for the districts' rebellion many years before.

Katniss and her fellow tribute from District Twelve, Peeta Mellark, win the Hunger Games by a combination of bravery, smarts, and a ploy of invoking sympathy from Capitol viewers (it's all televised) by pretending they are lovers. The degree of that pretense, of course, becomes blurred. Still, it works, and it allows them to be co-victors instead of the traditional single winner.

Ray-views

The second novel, *Catching Fire* finds Katniss and Peeta living in the Victor's Village back home in District Twelve where they are provided a nice house, money, and plenty of food. This granted affluence, however, requires them to make a victory tour of the districts, with the added pressure of continuing their "star-crossed lovers" act so as to convince the populace, and President Snow, that their winning ploy in the Hunger Games was done out of their desperate love and not in defiance of Capitol.

Their act doesn't go so well when they are not able to keep up an adequate pretense of support for Panem in the face of the suffering they see in their tour of the districts. This leads to President Snow deciding to eliminate them by picking the tributes for the next Hunger Games from the pool of previous year winners. So Katniss and Peeta have to fight for the second year in a row. Since they are up against previous winners, their odds for survival are even worse than last year, and they won't be allowed to share a victory this time.

Catching Fire continues the socialist theme begun in the first novel which makes it a stand-out in the popular fiction being produced today. It is still written at a Young Adult level but is complex enough to make it compelling to adult readers. In my opinion, Ms Collins has done a much better job with her prose in this book, which was a little too juvenile at points in the first. I also have to give her points for being a savvy storyteller. It would have been easy for her to make the succeeding books' plots surround the next year's Hunger Games (as in each *Harry Potter* book being another year at Hogwarts) but she continues her story instead and it makes for a single, strong piece of fiction.

Without giving anything away (there may be somebody out there that hasn't seen the movie), *Catching Fire* starts like another *Hunger Games* but with the twist of a competition among the previous winners. The ending, however, is forced by the rebellion against Capitol and the brave smarts of Katniss that cements her role as the rebellion's symbol. The book ends with an image of the next level of open rebellion, and an obvious pause in the storytelling. It begs not just for a sequel, but to continue the story.

Catching Fire is the continuation of *Hunger Games*, further developing characters, relationships, and situations in a satisfying and compelling way. It is the second part of an important story destined to become a classic in dystopian, populist literature.

Mockingjay

Author: Suzanne Collins
Publisher: Scholastic, Inc.
Publication date: 3/25/2014
Pages: 400
ISBN-13: 9780545663267
Type: Fiction, Science Fiction & Fantasy, Dystopian
Ray's rating: 5 stars
Characters: Katniss Everdeen, Peeta Mellark, Gale Hawthorne, Haymitch Abernathy, Caesar Flickerman, Effie Trinket

The first version of this review appeared on the www.goodreads.com website in January of 2014.

RAY-VIEW

MOCKINGJAY is the third novel in Suzanne Collins' *Hunger Games* dystopian trilogy. It is a high-action continuation of the story of Katniss Everdeen, the "girl on fire" who comes from an oppressed obscurity to become the inspiration for an armed rebellion against the source of that oppression, namely, the government of Panem centered in the city simply called, "Capitol."

Ms Collins' first two novels tell Katniss' story starting with her participation in the 74th annual Hunger Games, where she substituted for her little sister as a "tribute" in that highly-hyped and televised fight-to-the-death annual event. The games are a punishment of the Panem districts for their past rebellion, and amount to the sacrificial death of a boy and girl, aged 12 to 18, from each district. Katniss survived that year's games, along with her co-tribute Peeta, and emerged as a symbol of resistance for the districts. Panem's President Snow sought to squash that symbolism in the second novel (*Catching Fire*) by having past game "winners" be the tributes for the 75th Hunger Games. But those games were cut short by subterfuge from rebel forces in the districts (centered in District 13) and an act of insight and courage by Katniss. And so began the outright, armed rebellion of the districts that forms the backdrop of *Mockingjay*.

Mockingjay picks up right where second novel left off, with Katniss being swept away from the Hunger Games and Capitol by hovercraft to the center of rebel resistance in District 13. There she becomes a "media star," transformed by the propaganda wing of the rebels (with help from her former Hunger Games makeup team) into the "Mockingjay," complete with costume. She becomes the living symbol of the rebellion and makes propaganda videos that the rebel tech and former Hunger Games champion, Beetee, plays over the Capitol's television feed to all the districts. Her videos inspire the rebels to martial gains even as she continues to work out her emotional relationship with her childhood friend, Gale Hawthorne. That relationship is developed in triangle with Katniss' fellow-tribute, Peeta Mellark, who was taken prisoner by Capitol and then rescued, but returned in a shattered state.

The working out of that love triangle is not completed until the very end of the book, and by then Katniss' choice seems right and natural. Ms Collins handles that very well, and indeed, she handles everything very well in this book. There's a lot of action in this novel (much with a video game flavor), enough to provide material for the two movies done on it. Even so, Ms Collins doesn't lose her thread of Katniss' character through it all, which is admirable, otherwise her story would have fallen flat. All the fighting, suffering, and political machinations that Katniss goes through take their toll on her and we feel it as she carries on, wearing down into a black pit that it seems she will not escape from alive. This dynamic leads to a very satisfying ending (in terms of being believable and "right" within the context of the story being told) and was done so well that it prompted my award of a fifth star.

Another thing Ms Collins does well in all three books is to express the populist struggle of oppressed workers against their masters. I see her story as a *1984* and *Brave New World* for our times and I expect it, and the resultant movies, will join the ranks of classics in that literary genre. It is that political, human, aspect that, in my opinion, makes this story tower above other speculative, fantasy, action stories (YA or Adult). It is why I recommend the book so highly. I hope it will continue to avoid suppression and that young readers will see beyond the action and romance, and learn from its theme of class injustice that it mirrors so well from our times.

You see that mirror in Katniss' summation of the world she has come to know through all her trials:

But in the end, who does it benefit? No one. The truth is, it benefits no one to live in a world where these things happen.

There is so much truth in that.

Mockingjay

What impressed me most about *Mockingjay*, though, was its ending. And Ms Collins did *end* her epic, leaving no opening for continuation (without writing a totally different story). I believe she was right to do that, and in doing so she gave us an ending that is somberly touching, with just the right mixture of mellow sadness and hopeful highlights. Katniss is at the end of her journey, bearing awful scars--physical and emotional. We sympathize with her spiritual drain, having persevered with her through the three novels, and are still pulling for her even with the adventure completed. We want her to be OK as we take our leave. This is a good place to be at the end of an epic. It reminds me of the end of *The Lord of the Rings*, which has a long post-climax where you say goodbye to characters you've come to love.

So we say goodbye to Katniss and the other characters we've come so far with. These characters, bits of dialogue, situations and themes will come to mind as we long ponder this story. And we will, because it stays with us, speaking beyond the closing of the book's cover.

The Witch of Hebron: A World Made by Hand Novel

Author: James Howard Kunstler
Publisher: Grove/Atlantic, Inc.
Publication date: 9/27/2011
Pages: 336
ISBN-13: 9780802119612
Type: Fiction, Post Apocalyptic
Ray's rating: 4 stars
Characters: Lauren, Brother Job

The first version of this review appeared on the www.goodreads.com website in January of 2012.

RAY-VIEW

THE GREATEST value of this book (and its prequel, *World Made by Hand*), is the world it describes. That world is the community of Union Grove in the northeastern (former) US after the collapse of industrial civilization. What that collapse entails can be gleaned from Kunstler's nonfiction book, *The Long Emergency,* and from his weekly blog (www.kunstler.com), but its root lies in fossil fuel depletion ("Peak Oil"). The subsequent contraction has left people living at a roughly nineteenth century level amid the ruins of our high-tech society.

I've always loved stories set "after the apocalypse" and the two *World Made by Hand* novels are no exception. They are, I believe, very realistic and present a likely scenario based on current trends. If anything, Kunstler's predicted world may be too optimistic. Though life is hard in that his characters have to grow their own food, walk or ride horses to get around, and do without electricity (unless they can generate it themselves), and contend with lawlessness, they have formed viable communities and rediscovered living in cooperation with nature. Their lives are near-idyllic and I fear our future will be much harder than that. But then, Kunstler is really describing life in a pocket community that has no knowledge of what's going on in the wider world. And whatever that is, it has no influence on the town of Union Grove.

The main characters in *The Witch of Hebron* are mostly those from *World Made by Hand*, though there are some new ones with the promise

The Witch of Hebron

of storylines for future books. Some storylines are carried over from the first book, though they don't dominate, and there is an overarching murder mystery (sort of) that began in the first book and is not resolved in this one (or maybe it is, to the reader). Plot, however, is subordinate to environment in both books. It reminds me of James Fenimoore Cooper's *The Pioneers* in that respect—the description of the world at a particular time and how people live in it, being the author's main purpose.

The Witch of Hebron is a short novel with a lot of short chapters (74 and an epilogue). It is good writing, not great. I think time spent in more character development would have benefited the story, as well as a stronger main plot. Overall, it's a compilation of subplots and it isn't clear which will emerge as the main one until midway through. But then, Kunstler wasn't writing a thriller and I suspect that his short chapters and sparse prose is his comment on the attention spans of modern readers and the influence of television.

I'm rating *The Witch of Hebron* four out of five stars for its social statement and predictive value. It is a "must read" for that reason, rather than for it's literary merits.

Mr. Kunstler is a colorful, opinionated commentator and he holds back on all that in his *World Made by Hand* novels. That's good, though, because it makes these books more accessible to a general readership who would probably be put off by the overt cynicism of his blog and would more likely read *The Witch of Hebron* than *The Long Emergency*.

So I highly recommend *The Witch of Hebron* (but read *World Made by Hand* first) because it's more than "just a story." It's a picture of where we're going.

The Road

Author: Cormac McCarthy
Publisher: Knopf Doubleday Publishing Group
Publication date: 3/28/2007
Pages: 241
ISBN-13: 9780307387899
Type: Fiction, Post Apocalyptic
Ray's rating: 4 stars
Characters: The man, The boy

The first version of this review appeared on the www.goodreads.com website in April of 2012.

RAY-VIEW

THE ROAD, written by Cormac McCarthy, is a dark vision of a post-apocalyptic world. Where most stories of this genre offer some version of heroic survivors fighting marauders, aliens, mutants, or monsters in a revived, sun-drenched landscape or vacant cities, this story doesn't. The world is a charred ruin and nature won't produce. Human survivors fight over scraps. Heroism is subtle and hard to find beneath the overriding desperation and despair.

This is dark material for a Pulitzer prize winner, but for all that darkness, it is compelling. I was drawn to the nameless protagonist's journey across a desolate landscape, trying to get his son to a safe place that likely doesn't exist. But his single-minded determination out of love for his son keeps him going, and kept me reading.

I saw the movie version, starring Viggo Mortensen, a few years ago. It was a fine attempt and followed the book pretty well, but it didn't grab me the way the book did. I just found it depressing. I think this is a story best told in written prose since so much of it is the man's interior monologue and memories. Even the layout of the book supports the story.

The book is a long series of short paragraphs with no chapter breaks (though there are section breaks denoted by unobtrusive lines of three dots). The reading mirrors the man and boy's journey--unending with no stops, only rests. The prose is simple to the point of being stark, like the world around them. Even the punctuation is reduced, with no quotation marks around dialogue and little use of commas or apostrophes (especially

The Road

in contractions, so "won't" becomes "wont"). It's odd reading at first, but it works, and I had no trouble following the action or the dialogue.

The setting is the near future after some vague apocalyptic event, or series of events, that seems to have involved great fires because a gray ash is everywhere. It covers the ruined buildings, the ground, and is even mixed with the rain and snow, coloring the landscape in a depressing pallor. The ruination of humanity's constructed world is complemented by the ruination of nature. Nothing grows. There are few animals since most have either died from disease or been eaten. The human survivors live off what they can find, and off of each other. The man sees it as "The frailty of everything revealed at last."

With the inability to produce food and disease widespread, the futility of the situation is constantly apparent to those survivors able to think ahead. It leads many to give up and take their own lives. The man struggles with that temptation. An old man he meets on the road expresses this futility with the opinion that "Things will be better when everybody's gone."

So where's the hope in all this? What keeps the man from just killing himself and the boy?

There really is no hope for the survivors. Nobody has found a means to sustain themselves when the leftovers of the old world run out. McCarthy seems to be saying that when we're stripped of all support systems, sustenance, and hope, we are left only with existence. And the only meaning we can find in that existence is in love for each other.

There's precious little love among the survivors, but it burns brightly between the man and his young son. His love for the boy and determination to protect him from the evil around them is the only motivation he has left. It drives him down the road, his only destination being safety for the boy. And where that is, is as uncertain as everything else:

"Where are we going?"
"We're going south."

I'm giving *The Road* four stars because it has something important to say about the human condition, on a number of levels. It's not a "feel good" story, but it powerfully conveys the theme of keeping up the struggle even in the face of futility and misery. As the man says:

Ray-views

"When your dreams are of some world that never was or of some world that never will be and you are happy again then you will have given up. Do you understand? And you cant give up. I wont let you."

Hard words, but the boy needs to hear them. We need to hear them from time-to-time. Like a cold slap in the face, they keep us from falling asleep from the narcotic of our distractions. We need to stay awake and focused because there are others that depend on us.

We can't give up.

Visions of the Future

Source: Ray's Journal, www.rayfoy.com, 08-Apr-2012

MY WIFE and I recently saw the movie, *The Hunger Games*. I've not read the book, but I was very interested in the story based on a review I had read. My wife has read the trilogy and loved it. Well, the movie was great and I hope to read the books at some point. I was most impressed with Suzanne Collins' commentary on current American society expressed in a dystopian story.

I also finished reading *The Road* (by Cormac McCarthy) which is more apocalyptic than dystopian and presents a bleaker future for humanity than *The Hunger Games*. *The Road* is brilliant in that it studies humans trying to survive in a state of total loss. It provides a dark alternate view of the post apocalypse than is the fictional usual.

These stories represent a growing body of works that seem only able to speculate about a future that is politically totalitarian and environmentally desolate. I think we're seeing so many such stories because thoughtful people are seeing little hope for humanity. I know that when I try to do a serious depiction of the future, I find I can only extrapolate oppression from our rulers and a great degradation of the natural environment. Anything else really *is* fantasy.

But despite their pessimistic thesis, there is hope in both of these stories. *The Hunger Games* protagonist and her friends see the evil of the ruling powers and even contemplate rebellion. Even thinking about opposing evil is hope. Indeed, promoting, controlling, and suppressing hope for a better life is a major theme of the story. A large part of our cheering for Katniss in her struggles is our hope of her people opposing and overcoming the totalitarian "Capitol."

The hope in *The Road* is more subtle. The man and the boy are going south to escape the evil and death that is all around them. Their hope is based only on their desire to get away from their present dangers, rather than any concrete knowledge that the dangers are truly less elsewhere. But the man and boy are together, which is their only consolation, and they act out of love for each other, which is the foundation of their hope. They hang on in the face of near-certain death. Their hope for better in the south is a faith in things not seen.

Which story represents a more likely vision of the future? Well, I expect the truth will fall somewhere in between. I think *The Hunger Games* is a fair representation of our present, and *The Road* is a more likely the representation of our future.

Both stories are considerations of our futures, though for different dramatic purposes. Both are bleak but with different ideas of where hope lies. *The Hunger Games* sees hope for our future as being determined by our actions, especially our collective actions. *The Road* sees hope as limited and based on luck since our supporting environment is destroyed.

Our hope for facing an uncertain, even threatening, future may well rest on our own resolve and the ability of nature to continue to support us; also luck and faith. I think all of it will be needed to get humanity through the next century.

Suggested for Further Reading

Why I Write by George Orwell (Eric Blair)

The Shadow Masters by Daniel Estulin

Heart of Darkness by Joseph Conrad

Crossing the Rubicon by Michael C. Ruppert

The Party's Over by Richard Heinberg

The World Without Us by Alan Weisman

Ray-views

Inspiration

INSPIRATION is what gets us from one day to the next--from one moment to the next. Though there are common themes, what inspires one person or another is as unique as a fingerprint. That singleness of inspiration comes from the associations people make over the course of their lives with the impressions they constantly receive. Impressions of form, color, feeling, songs, words, joy, fear, fatigue, exhilaration, desire, desolation, comfort, anxiety, love, and hate. All the permutations of these and others that we perceive in our observations and experiences, form a reservoir from which we draw out emotional constructs. When we draw out the best ones, we are inspired.

We crave our inspirations. We yearn for them, surround ourselves with reminders of them, and follow rituals that keep them in front of us. That's why we have favorite books and movies, favorite foods and favorite places we visit. Our need to be inspired is so great that sometimes we live in a constant rush from one inspiration to another. People who live that way are often called, thrill-seekers. Their lives can be awe-inspiring, but they run the risk of getting lost in delusion and of not having a firm enough emotional grounding should their inspirations prove false, or simply change.

Because life is constantly in motion, so are our inspirations. They can fade or grow stronger. Very often, they morph into something else. This is why inspirations need to be renewed. It's why churches have revivals and corporations have employee "Spring Flings" and "Team Building." It's all dealing with life's impermanence and searching for a way to keep going.

That search can be an actual journey. There is something about exposing yourself to the rigors of a physical trek--making yourself vulnerable to the elements so you can find your strengths and figure out what you need to do. And so all but one of the stories in this category involves a journey of some sort. These journeys are usually prompted by a need to find something--something lost, something required to recover from failure, or something desperately desired. In all cases the characters or narrators, in finding their way down a physical path, are also finding their way in life.

Ray-views

Because this idea of finding inspiration is so visceral to the human experience, many literary classics are "journey stories." Consider *The Odyssey* and *The Lord of the Rings*. They never lose their appeal. That's also why long treks through specific places have developed over human history and remain as well-known religious pilgrimages. As Paulo Coelho says in *The Pilgrimage*:

> *...a religious pilgrimage has always been one of the most objective ways of achieving insight.*

Mr. Coelho was thinking specifically about the Santiago de Compostela Camino in northern Spain. That is a very old religious pilgrimage and may even predate Christianity. He is one of many to undertake the 500 mile hike and write about it. His pilgrimage was very much a nonreligious but spiritual undertaking, and was also a test of his character by an esoteric society that he belonged to. It was a redemptive journey for him, and he was guided by a mentor who was deliberately shaping it towards a specific end for Mr. Coelho.

Shirley MacLaine, the actress, also walked the Camino. She was 65 years old at the time. Her reasons were less specific than Mr. Coelho's. She was simply seeking to find whatever insights there were to find in making the attempt. Still, she did her homework first and understood the reason most people make the pilgrimage. She says in her book, *The Camino*:

> *The experience of complete surrender to God and self is the motivation behind most people's attempt at the Santiago de Compostela Camino.*

In her own surrendering to the Camino, Ms MacLaine experienced some past-life visions that constituted her personal insight. Being a spiritual seeker, she was looking for metaphysical inspiration from the start (or at least was open to it). Others undertake pilgrimages that are less established, nonrelgious, and they go with only the hope for insight.

In trying to find her way through the despair and loss of her life's emotional anchor, Cheryl Strayed defined her own personal pilgrimage through her serendipitous discovery of the Pacific Crest Trail. Her chancing upon a PCT guidebook prompted a chain of thought and emotion that led her to undertake the 1100 mile hike as a therapy. She had taken a blow from her mother's death that left her emotionally injured. In hiking the PCT, she was offering to the universe that surrender

Inspiration

of self that Ms MacLaine defined as the motivation for Camino pilgrims. She says in her book, *Wild*:

> *The wanting was a wilderness and I had to find my own way out of the woods...I didn't know where I was going until I got there...It was a place called the Bridge of the Gods.*

The Bridge of the Gods is a real bridge in Oregon and Ms Strayed's selected destination. When she got there, she also found that she had arrived at another place in life.

The other book in this category that describes a deliberate journey of inspiration is Mr. Coelho's little parable, *The Alchemist*. It's a fiction obviously inspired by the Camino, as indicated in the protagonist's name being "Santiago." A dream of "hidden treasure" buried at the Egyptian pyramids prompts Santiago to undertake a journey to find it. Of course, he finds treasure along the way in the spiritual sense, but he doesn't really appreciate its value until the end. Though he begins with different motives, he ends up in the same inspired place as Mr. Coelho, Ms MacLaine, and Ms Strayed.

The pilgrimages described in the above four books were undertaken deliberately by the authors (or the fictional protagonist). They all undertook the hardships of their journeys with the intention, or at least the strong hope, of finding the inspirations they needed or the rewards they desired. Others undertake their journey by accident. Circumstances thrust them upon a road they react to by seeking escape. In their struggles, they find their inspiration.

Like *The Alchemist*, Yann Martel's *Life of Pi* is as much parable as story, though it is longer with more involved plotting. Because of this, its nature as a parable is not so obvious until the end, where it becomes unclear how much of Pi's story is real. He even relates different versions of what happened to him. In any case, his stories reveal much about religion--what it is, what it says about God and man, and the relationship between the two. This has to do with inspiration, and in *Life of Pi*, Mr. Martel gives a brief, but stunning description of the insight found by seekers on their journeys:

> *...I suddenly felt I was in heaven. The spot was in fact no different from when I had passed it not long before, but my way of seeing it had changed.*

This is the same insight expressed by T. S. Eliot when he said seekers will return to the start of their journeys and "know the place for the first time." The place has not changed, but the journey has done its work on the journeyer.

Sometimes, the inspiration doesn't come on the journey itself, but at a place revealed along the way. Physically, that place is usually the destination, but even after getting there, the protagonist still has a way to go to reach his or her place of insight. That is the case with James Hilton's *Lost Horizon*. Mr. Hilton's characters embark on their journey completely against their will. While escaping by airplane from an attack by rebels, they are hijacked and taken to the Tibetan lamasery of Shangra La.

Shangra La shines its inspiration on the four westerners, but each receives it in a different way. Some want to stay and some want to leave, with differing levels of ardency. I see this as a picture of how inspirations affect us differently, even though they come from the same source experience.

Lost Horizon is one of my most favorite novels because it is about the appreciation of beauty, learning, compassion, and living in harmony with nature as being among the finer aspects of life. This appreciation exists in the shadow of a brutal world that does not value such fragile things. Our most cherished inspirations are fragile in the face of a might-makes-right world.

The protagonists of *Lost Horizon* find their inspiration in a place at their physical journey's end (and so are inspired to continue their individual journeys at a higher level). The same is true for the protagonist, Dr. Singh, in Ann Patchett's *State of Wonder*. Dr. Singh travels to a place in South America that is as alien to her as Shangra La, and not as hospitable.

In a South American jungle, Dr. Singh is searching for a lost associate and the answer to a mystery concerning human longevity. In the process, she wrestles with much physical discomfort, culture shocks, and even life-threatening dangers. In the midst of all this, however, inspiration is revealed that leads to her insights. She reaches the point where a stinging cloud of insects parts to reveal a night full of stars such as she never saw in her previous, more civilized life. Inspiration does come to us that way, suddenly and out of a cloud of discomfort or even fear. This is because there are many layers to life, and we generally see only the surface of things. All the while we are suffering, or distracted by problems, other dynamics are percolating that will certainly bring changes.

The other book by Ms Patchett in this category, *Run*, does not concern a physical journey. If a journey is involved at all, it is one of people coming together who have been separated. In the process, though, we see the characters acting upon their own inspirations. Indeed, that is a major theme of the novel. Ms Patchett seems to be making the point that

Inspiration

we must follow our own callings--scientific, religious, athletic, political--but still love and respect each other, because we are family.

And then it's helpful to consider old inspirations. As we grow older and change our attitudes, our inspirations will likely change as well. This is as it should be, and when we look back at what inspired us in our youth, we can see how far we've come and what we've left behind, lost, or simply outgrown. I got that feeling of "nostalgic inspiration" when I finally read the novel version of *2001: A Space Odyssey* by Arthur C. Clarke. My Rayview tells you what I think about the story, how it compares to the movie, etc. I also comment on that feeling of "high-tech reaching for the stars" that touched me and so many baby-boomers in the midst of the 1960s "space race." This was well before personal computers and the Internet, so we found our space travel fixes in movies, novels, TV shows (*Star Trek*), and news reports on NASA's moon program. It was heady stuff at the time and a lot of young boys wanted to grow up to be astronauts (girls too, I suppose, but "women's lib" was still building steam). And the general consensus was that it was important to "beat" the Russians to the moon. Nobody ever really said why.

A great pride came from this inspiration. With our technology, we humans would "conquer space" by colonizing the moon and Mars. There were resources to be exploited on both that would further fuel our expansion into the solar system and on to the stars. That was then. Now, NASA sends people only to low-earth orbit and only sends little robots to Mars and the other planets. It seems there is money enough only for war-making on Earth, and Earth will be all exploited-out before people ever leave her again. So if there's anything to be learned from this old inspiration, it appears to be a lesson taken from the gap that separates the original vision and the present reality.

You can find much to inspire in all the books in this category, but they are certainly not the final word in inspiration. Their value to you will depend on the associations that they prompt. As such, they are only samples. You will have your own list of inspirational books, movies, songs, etc. You should take that inspiration as a help to carry on, but don't try to go from thrill-to-thrill with no consideration for anything else. The thrills will always end because life is impermanent. If you can understand that, and appreciate the fragility of the better, finer, aspects of life, it may be that you find your inspiration remains with you, wherever you go.

The Alchemist

Author: Paulo Coelho
Publisher: HarperCollins Publishers
Publication date: 4/15/2014
Pages: 208
ISBN-13: 9780062315007
Type: Fiction, Personal Growth, Religion and Spirituality
Ray's rating: 4 stars
Characters: Santiago, Melchizedek, The crystal merchant, The Englishman, The Alchemist

The first version of this review appeared on the www.goodreads.com website in July of 2014.

RAY-VIEW

THE ALCHEMIST by Paulo Coelho is a little book rich in inspiration and in hope. Mr. Coelho says he wrote it from his soul, and that it is his metaphor for living.

Though it tells a story, *The Alchemist* is written as parable. The storyline is that of the Spanish shepherd boy, Santiago, who became a shepherd because he likes to travel (shepherds move their flocks around a lot, between pastures and markets). Though young (late teens apparently, though we're never told his age) he appreciates the mystery of life and the beauty of the natural world. One night, sleeping in the ruins of a sacred place, he dreams of a treasure buried somewhere in the vicinity of the Egyptian pyramids. He is greatly moved by this dream and believes it is an omen, so he sets out to find the treasure.

In the telling of Santiago's quest, Mr. Coelho presents many truisms and wise words through the voices of his characters and through their actions. He does this very well and it is like reading an extended version of your favorite teaching stories from Plato or from the Bible, or even an extensive work like *Don Quixote*. This makes *The Alchemist* very quotable, but the reader should understand this before delving into the book. Though Mr. Coelho tells his tale in a way that is more relatable for modern readers than the older works I mentioned, it is not written as a contemporary novel. It is not a George Martin or John Grisham or James Patterson story. I think this makes it a disappointment for some readers, but I consider it to be the book's great strength.

The Alchemist

Santiago's quest for the hidden treasure is his "Personal Legend," which he learns is an alchemical term for "what you have always wanted to accomplish." It is a consuming desire beyond the mere acquisition of stuff or power. It is recognizing that principal that controls all things, known in alchemy as the "Soul of the World." You recognize your place as a part of all things and acknowledge the guidance of the universe in fulfilling your Personal Legend. But realizing what your Personal Legend is, is not the hard part. It is pursuing it.

...when you really want something, it's because that desire originated in the soul of the universe. It's your mission on earth...And, when you want something, all the universe conspires in helping you to achieve it.

Santiago seeks verification for his dream-inspired quest and finds it in the words of a fortune-teller. So now he is seeking his treasure in earnest and finds help from several persons along the way. Each of these characters represent aspects of following our Personal Legend and provide their lessons to Santiago.

The first helper is Melchizedek, the King of Salem from the Bible. Melchizedek represents opportunity that requires a price. He tells Santiago that he always appears to seekers, though not always as a person. He could simply be "a solution, or a good idea." He tells Santiago where he will find his treasure and gives him advice on how to proceed in his journey. His advice, however, is at the cost of one tenth of Santiago's sheep (echoing the story in Genesis 14 where Melchizedek took a tenth of Abraham's war spoils in return for a blessing).

Later, Santiago encounters the crystal merchant. The merchant represents opportunity lost or ignored. He has remained with familiarity rather than take the risk of seeking his Personal Legend. Santiago's willingness to take the risk inspires the merchant to help, but at the cost of distress for the merchant because it makes him face his own lost opportunities. He tells Santiago that we are most regretful about those things we didn't do.

Then Santiago meets a fellow seeker who is an Englishman. This man is very intelligent and carries a load of books around with him. He has learned from his studies that the path to wisdom lies in understanding alchemy. He is smart enough to realize that his knowledge of alchemy is "book knowledge" and that he needs a master to teach him the operational side of the craft. He is a scientific seeker, but an open-minded one. He has much knowledge, and seeking to understand alchemy is his Personal Legend, but he needs "heart" to go further.

Ray-views

Finally, Santiago and the Englishman find the Alchemist, who is the master the Englishman has been seeking. This fierce man, living alone in the desert, represents the Personal Legend realized. His skills appear magical, but they are solidly based in being cooperative with nature. He puts it this way when asked:

> *"What is an alchemist?"* he asked, finally.
> *"It's a man who understands nature and the world..."*

The Alchemist has found his treasure. Now he seeks disciples to teach. He gives the Englishman a task to help him along, but takes a more personal involvement with Santiago. He intends to help the boy find his treasure. This help involves crossing the Sahara with a caravan and facing tribal war and bandits.

In this journey, Santiago endures many hardships but finds a desert girl who might be his future wife. Then he is challenged, upon pain of death, to turn himself into wind. He gets through it all and finally arrives at the Egyptian pyramids where his treasure is buried.

In telling Santiago's story, Mr. Coelho does not make the way easy for him. This story is a metaphor for living life and so he shows us Santiago's uncertainties, mistakes, and hardships. Like Don Quixote, Santiago takes a bashing several times. He also loses all he has gained (materially speaking, that is, his money) three times. So it is clear that monetary wealth is not the standard for judging success in pursuing your Personal Legend.

I read the 25th anniversary edition of *The Alchemist* which is illustrated with drawings that struck me as having a 19th century flavor that I found appealing. They are scattered throughout the book and compliment the narrative.

I expect I'll read *The Alchemist* again and again, and think about it often. It is a book that encourages thoughtful consideration long after its covers are closed. It is one of my favorite reads and a significant guidepost for anyone seeking to find and follow their Personal Legend.

The Camino: A Journey of the Spirit

Author: Shirley MacLaine
Publisher: Atria Books
Publication date: 4/1/2001
Pages: 320
ISBN-13: 9780743400732
Type: Nonfiction, Travel, Religion and Spirituality, Mysticism
Ray's rating: 4 stars

The first version of this review appeared on the www.goodreads.com website in August of 2012.

RAY-VIEW

I READ Shirley MacLaine's *The Camino* several years ago and it touched me in subtle ways as did her earlier book, *Out on a Limb*. This review is from my latest reread and trying to find that point of connection that had moved me so. Or maybe *points of connection*, for there are many.

First, Shirley MacLaine is no ordinary movie star. She is a capable writer, able to tell her story in engaging and intelligent prose, even when the subject matter is strange. She is aware of her privileged position that allows her to travel the world without the concerns that hinder the rest of us. Yet, she isn't so "full of herself" that she doesn't recognize that driving desire for *knowing* that marks her as a sincere seeker of knowledge and understanding, way beyond the illusions of fortune and fame.

The Camino is an apt telling of a journey undertaken by Ms MacLaine physically and spiritually. She tells a story that is an engaging travelogue highlighted with spiritual connotations that inspire and enlarge the recounting of her physical traveling. Her tale is also metaphorical, told with meaning for herself and her readers. She tells us about her spiritual journey that happened in the same space as the physical, and what it taught her. Her implication is that we can draw similar insight from our own life journeying.

In the introduction, she tells us what the Camino is:

> There is a famous pilgrimage that has been taken by people for centuries called the Santiago de Compostela Camino across northern Spain. It is said that the Camino -- the road or the way -- lies directly under the Milky Way and follows ley lines that reflect the energy from those star systems above it.

Ray-views

Then she gives us the reason people undertake the grueling, 500 mile, pilgrimage:

The Santiago Camino...is done with the intent to find one's deepest spiritual meaning and resolutions regarding conflicts in Self.

With this intent toward spiritual self-discovery, Ms MacLaine launched her own journey down that ancient way prompted by anonymous letters sent to her while she was doing performances in South America. With further encouragement from spiritually-minded friends, she undertook the trek in 1994 when she was in her sixties. Just making such a trip at that time in her life is an inspiration for those of us wondering how many trips we have left in us.

She relates how she started her pilgrimage in Saint-Jean-Pied-de-Port in France, crossed the Pyrenees mountains into Spain, and walked village-to-village, staying in sordid little *refugios* (places for Camino pilgrims to stay the night) until she reached her journey's end at the town of Santiago de Compostela. Along the way she faced territorial dogs, rain, sometimes annoying fellow pilgrims, cold showers, intrusive paparazzi, self-serving priests, and persistent dreams of her past lives, always urged on by the locals with the exhortation of: *Ultreya!* -- move forward with courage.

Sleeping in the refugios, in the open, or sometimes in a hotel, she dreamed. At times, her dreams were so lucid she considered them visions, and they were all about her past lives. Indeed, her telling of those past-life visions of traveling the Camino in the Middle Ages and of living in Atlantis and in Lemuria are what puts this book solidly in the "New Age" section of the book store. Enhanced by the concentrated energy of the Camino, many of her visions were of traveling on the Camino as a Moorish girl, apparently a mistress to Charlemagne, as a pupil of "John the Scot" (who is also one of her chief spirit guides). Others were of her as an androgynous being in Lemuria and Atlantis who was an early experiment carried out by aliens on the sexual separation of humans. The latter is an image of humanity's "split" from it's previous state of unity (between yin and yang) to its current state of disconnection, ever seeking its other half.

Such visions will be off-putting to many, but they should not be so quick to judge. While I personally don't believe there was a real Lemuria and Atlantis with aliens that sank into the ocean, I do believe they are powerful and persistent metaphors of our civilization and the dangers of arrogant materialism. They warn us of the inevitable collapse from living

The Camino: A Journey of the Spirit

the way we do. They go along with ecological themes of preserving the earth and creating sustainable modes of living, rather than the paradigm of "endless growth." Such themes are constant at the core of mystical lore, and Shirley MacLaine's works are no exception. Indeed, while she avers the reality of having had the visions, she still alludes to them as being instructive imaginings.

In *The Camino*, Ms MacLaine says:

Without the recognition of the soul's journey within us, we are lost and only part of what we were intended to be.

Maybe finding that lost part of us is the attraction in "journey" stories that make them classics, like *The Odyssey*, *The Lord of the Rings* and even *Gulliver's Travels*. I know that, in spite of the "fantastic" parts, I've been able to relate to Shirley MacLaine's writings in my own quest for enlightenment because I recognize in her prose the quest for understanding of a fellow seeker. And so I highly recommend *The Camino* to you as a guidepost to help you in your own journey through this mysterious life.

Ultreya!

Life of Pi

Author: Yann Martel
Publisher: Mariner Books
Publication date: 05/01/2003
Pages: 326
ISBN-13: 978-0156027328
Type: Fiction, Psychological, Action and Adventure
Ray's rating: 5 stars
Characters: Piscine Molitor Patel (Pi), Richard Parker - the Bengal Tiger, Francis Adirubasamy, Ravi, Santosh Patel, Satish Kumar, Father Martin, Satish Kumar

The first version of this review appeared on the www.goodreads.com website in September of 2014.

RAY-VIEW

LIFE OF PI is one of those stories that strikes readers at multiple levels as they read it, but like a fine wine, reveals its complexity in after-tastes of reflection. It is, at one level, a story about survival at sea, though with a twist--the castaway, Pi, shares his lifeboat with an adult Bengal tiger! Obviously, this adds layers to the adversity Pi must struggle against to survive and it is the dominant "taste" of the story. This core narrative is engaging and the author, Yann Martel, apparently did his research on ocean survival very well because this aspect of his novel is believable. He also seems to know a lot about animal behavior, especially tigers, from the standpoint of zookeepers, and was able to integrate that knowledge into an ocean castaway story. All that is quite a feat, and it works.

But *Life of Pi* is not just a "lost at sea" survival story. It is about religion. It explores what religion is, what it means to people, and how it stands in relation to faith, hope, spiritual epiphany, and even fear. Pi's "uncle" tells a journalist that Pi's story is one that will make you believe in God. It might. It will certainly make you think about God, and examine your beliefs, or lack thereof, about Him/Her.

Life of Pi is told in three parts within an encompassing frame. The frame tells the story of the author (a story character, but it seems to be Mr. Martel playing himself) discovering Pi's story from a family friend of Pi in India (referred to as an "uncle"). The friend, Mr. Adirubasamy, directs the author to find Pi in Toronto. The author, intrigued by what

Life of Pi

the man has told him, does search out Pi and interviews him. That interview process is told briefly in short, italicized chapters in the book's first part. These sections serve as a frame for more than just story construction. They also frame the story's themes that I take as: "most people miss the better sides of life," and, "the central core of all religions." Both are expressed early in a passage where the author speaks of his most recent interview session with Pi:

Our encounters always leave me weary of the glum contentment that characterizes my life...What of God's silence?...An intellect confounded yet a trusting sense of presence and of ultimate purpose.

As for Pi's story, it begins with Pi as a teenaged Indian boy in the small town of Pondicherry in India. His full name is Piscine Molitor Patel and he tells us that he was named after a famous swimming pool. He is given grief for his name in school (his first name is pronounced with a small 'i' sound in the first syllable). He resolves the problem with a typical ingenuity that serves him well later when he is lost at sea. He shortens his name to 'Pi' (with a long 'i' sound) and makes the association of it to the math concept (3.14). This effectively dispels the negative association that was making him the butt of jokes.

Pi's father is a zookeeper and so Pi grows up around all kinds of wild animals within the zoo environment. Pi develops his own passion for animals and zoo-keeping and it leads him to make zoology part of his double major in college. The other major is religion, which he also develops a passion for in Pondicherry. Pi describes his encounters there with holy men of the Christian, Muslim, and Hindu faiths that lead him to embrace all three religions. Indeed, he practices all three unabashedly (but in secret from his parents, who are basically atheists).

Pi is able to express his faith and "trusting sense of presence and ultimate purpose" through these three major religions. To him, God is not limited to any one of them. This view is underscored by two beautiful images in the book's first part. The first is when the local clerics of these religions meet Pi and his family while on a Sunday stroll. When they realize that Pi is a faithful follower of all of their religions, they are astounded. They cannot accept that a person can be a Catholic, a Muslim, and a Hindu without contradiction and they argue violently about it.

The second image is when Pi is showing two wise men around his father's zoo. One man is an atheist and the other is a Muslim. With Pi, the realist, they view a Grant's zebra and all express their appreciation of the

Ray-views

animal's beauty from their own perspective. They are together in their differences with no arguments at all.

With this foundation of thought about religion in the first part, Mr. Martel takes us into the second which is the story of Pi's ordeal as a castaway. It is easy to see the second part as an illustration of the first in the form of a detailed and intense parable, and that's just how I took it.

The setting for the second part is mostly the Pacific Ocean. Pi and his family, with their zoo, are relocating to Canada. The old cargo ship they are traveling on sinks, putting Pi into his lifeboat situation with the tiger. The tiger is named, "Richard Parker." The reason given for the unusual name is a believable little tidbit and it works to emphasize the tiger as more of a personal force in the story than if he had been named, "Twinkie" or some such.

Pi's journey across the Pacific with Richard Parker is an engrossing tale with powerful images to ponder. The sea, with all its majesty of sheer expanse, brimming with life, alternating between bounty and dearth in providing Pi with food, fierce storms, days of beauty and days of boredom, is surely an image of life. Pi travels it with the tiger that he must train if he is to make the voyage safely (we all have our tigers to tame). But safety is elusive and false versions present themselves several times, including a carnivorous island. I had to ponder the point of the carnivorous island and all I can decide is that it's something like Odysseus' time on the island of the Lotus-eaters, where his men just wanted to stay happy and drugged with no thought of continuing their journey home.

Several times, Pi reaches the point in his long, arduous, struggle where he is just worn out and feeling hopeless and alone. It is at these points that he says he turns to God:

> *I grew weary of my situation, as pointless as the weather. But life would not leave me. The rest of this story is nothing but grief, ache and endurance...It was natural that, bereft and desperate as I was, in the throes of unremitting suffering, I should turn to God...Solitude began. I turned to God. I survived.*

At the times Pi says this about "turning to God," he offers no further comment on the matter. He does not explain in what way he "turns to God." I think the examination of Pi's religious development in the first part answers that, or begins to. And I think at these times that Pi is rediscovering "God's silence" and perhaps the "still, small voice" that is the place where God is always found.

It is in those times that come so regularly in our lives, when we are suffering the agonies of pain or boredom or pointlessness, and we are

Life of Pi

overcome with despair, that we are pushed to turn to whatever we consider the higher power. While all such considerations are unique, they are also all the same, and they provide the same service.

I won't give away any spoilers as to Pi's "rescue" or of the action in the third part. Just let me say that it leaves no doubt that the story is indeed about religion. It underscores the role of "story" in our religious beliefs and the importance of the stories we embrace in getting us through life.

I believe that with *Life of Pi*, Yann Martel has produced a classic work of literature for the twenty-first century. If there are any open-minded classrooms in the future, surely Mr. Martel's book will be required reading for them. It is a book that I highly recommend for the serious student of life. It will help mold your thinking about the story you prefer, and maybe help you find it, whether you are atheist, Catholic, Muslim, or Hindu.

Lost Horizon

Author: James Hilton
Publisher: Pocket Books, a division of Simon and Schuster, Inc
Publication date: first published in June 1933
Pages: 231
ISBN: 0-671-66427-1
Type: Fiction, Religion and Spirituality, Action and Adventure
Ray's rating: 5 stars
Characters: Hugh Conway, Chalmers Bryant, Lo-Tsen, Malison

The first version of this review appeared on the www.goodreads.com website in October of 2013.

RAY-VIEW

I HAD to read *Lost Horizon* three times, over a number years, to really appreciate it. It is a story that is subtle in its sophistication, much like a fine wine. Though set in pre-World War II years (it was first published in 1933) with a strong male protagonist, it is not an *Indiana Jones* type adventure. While the excitement of travel is a theme, the action is not rip-roaring, it is internal and complex. Conflicts are not between good-guys and bad-guys, but between differing agendas and desires, and from perceptions of duty vs personal need. Yet it is not a deep, psychological study either. Rather, Mr. Hilton seems to have had some points he wanted to make by means of some particular themes and depictions, and he did so, very well.

Mr. Hilton opens his book with one such picture that he repeats throughout the story. Three men are in a British embassy sitting room, smoking cigars, and discussing a mystery. That mystery concerns what happened to an airplane that disappeared with four passengers aboard during the evacuation of the Indian town of Baskul, which was under attack by rebels. Aboard the plane was a British Consul named Hugh Conway. The men all knew Conway, to one degree or other, and all agree he was a remarkable, clever fellow, though "rather slack." His fate, and that of his three companions, is unknown.

Later, two of the men, the unnamed narrator and Rutherford, a novelist, retire to Rutherford's hotel room where they continue the conversation in another sitting room (with more drinks and cigars). Rutherford tells the narrator that he actually encountered Conway at a

Lost Horizon

hospital in Chung-Kiang, a few months before. There, and later on a voyage they shared from Shanghai to Honolulu, he obtained an amazing story from Conway concerning the hijacked flight from Baskul and subsequent events. Rutherford wrote a manuscript of Conway's story, which he provides to the narrator whose reading of it constitutes the story of *Lost Horizon*. Here the narrative shifts back to those events as seen from Conway's viewpoint.

In the midst of the rebel assault on Baskul, Conway and his companions are kidnapped and taken by airplane to a very remote part of Tibet. There, they are met by a party that takes them to a lamasery called, Shangri-La. The place is dominated by the mountain, Karakal, and is sheltered from the harsh elements by peaks that rival Everest in height. Shangri-La is huge, with gardens, courtyards, a library stocked with many European works, and even musical instruments with stores of classical compositions (some unknown to the world). It is supported by a village nestled in the valley below that grows food in abundance due to its sheltered location. There is also much gold there, mined to support the lamasery's purchases of items from the outside world.

Shangri-La is paradise--a peaceful, contemplative place, where physical and spiritual needs are well met. Dealing with it all is the challenge for Conway and his companions, and they do so in their own ways. The reader sees that what constitutes paradise is very much in the eye of the beholder.

In my first readings of *Lost Horizon*, I was uncertain of the story's point and was somewhat put off by the lack of a black-and-white conflict (where are the Nazis, the zombies, or even the yetis?). This likely came from my conditioning by the over-hyped, over-tech'ed, entertainments of our time. I suspect that's a problem for a lot of contemporary readers. Age, however, seems to have tempered my conditioning and allowed me, in this last reading, to appreciate, and greatly enjoy, the novel's low-key intensity.

That subtle intensity is exemplified in the character of Hugh Conway. He has the image of a "take charge" hero and he impresses people with his intelligence and strength--so much so that his associates call him "Glory Conway" and wonder why he hasn't risen higher in government service. His job is that of British Consul and he has never gotten the desirable assignments that could have helped his career (he is thirty seven at the time of the story events). We find out that his image is just that--an image--and Conway has been very deliberate in creating it because it is helpful in maintaining his job. Conway is capable in his career, but unmotivated. This is the worker's dilemma and Conway states it simply and brilliantly in conversation with the Shangri-La High Lama:

It always seemed to me in my profession that a good deal of what passed for success would be rather disagreeable, apart from needing more effort than I felt called upon to make...

Amen, brother. Our corporate masters condemn such an attitude as lazy, and our fellow workers readily take up the cry. They willingly, even arrogantly, sacrifice their time--their lives--to their jobs. They even provide their own electronic irons to bind themselves to their oars. The High Lama comments:

Laziness in doing stupid things can be a great virtue...

Shangri-La is a product of brilliant minds and enlightened souls that shatter Conway's delusions and entice him to abandon the outside world with it's desires for destruction, and rest in a harbor of art and learning and mindful sophistication. Conway is drawn to all this while his vice consul, Mallison, is not. We see this in both of them falling in love with Lo-Tsen, the young Manchu girl who frequently entertains at Shangri-La with piano recitals. Conway's love is from afar, appreciating her grace and her musical eloquence. Mallison's love is more immediate and carnal. Love flowers for them both, but produces differing blossoms.

The difference in Conway and Mallison's relations to Lo-Tsen--indeed, to Shangri-La itself--is in large part a function of where each is in their life's journey. Mallison is young and eager to get on with living, so he can't stand the slow pace of Shangri-La. Conway is nearing mid-life, having been broken and disillusioned by the first world war. In this, he is almost a Joseph Conrad antihero, but he is not beyond redemption and he believes he has found it in this place, evidenced by his appreciation of Lo-Tsen.

The great theme of *Lost Horizon* is, to me, the consideration of what paradise means to each of us; how we deal with it if we find it or create it, and how it can survive in a dark, destructive world. Mr. Hilton explores the possibilities for the personal part in the reactions to Shangri-La of his characters. His answer to the survival part he puts in the words of the High Lama:

We may expect no mercy, but we may faintly hope for neglect.

Lost Horizon

In other words, "let's hope they don't notice us," for knowledge of Shangri-La by the outer world would surely bring about the lamasery's destruction. These days, Shangri-La would be hyped and trivialized, and treated as a reality show. A celebrity would shoot a cable channel episode there, remark on it's beauty, simple foods, thin air, and declare the stories of long-lived lamas to be superstition. Corporations would fight over its gold.

But no book is perfect and I have a few criticisms of *Lost Horizon*. I thought the secondary characters, especially Barnard and Miss Brinklow, were too one-dimensional. Though Mr. Hilton made his points for each in their relations to Shangri-La, I believe those points would have been better made by showing more facets of their characters and personal stories. Also, he should have explored more of Shangri-La itself in his narrative. The lamasery's wonder is conveyed more in the words of the characters than in the reader's feeling it through the prose. That is, we know Shangri-La is beautiful because the characters say it is, rather than "seeing" it through the prose. A good balance there would only have enhanced the storytelling.

At the end of the book, the narrative returns to the original narrator and Rutherford, where we find them drinking and smoking again and discussing the implications of Conway's story. They also must decide their own reactions to it. For the readers of *Lost Horizon* to do the same was, I think, Mr. Hilton's intention and is likely why the book is such a classic. It is certainly one of my favorite books of all time.

The Pilgrimage

Author: Paulo Coelho
Publisher: HarperCollins e-books
Publication date: 10/13/2009
Pages: 272
ASIN: B000JMKNZG
Type: Nonfiction, Spiritual Growth, Travel
Ray's rating: 4 stars
Characters: Paulo Coelho, Petrus

The first version of this review appeared on the www.goodreads.com and www.booklikes.com websites in April of 2015.

RAY-VIEW

THE PILGRIMAGE is the story of Paulo Coelho's experience of walking the ancient road to Santiago in northern Spain (the Santiago de Compostela Camino). He presents his tale as a true story (and I believe it is true that Mr. Coelho walked the Camino) but it contains some strong esoteric (i.e., paranormal) elements that struck me as "embellished for effect." Even so, the story is another strong recounting of a seeker making this ancient pilgrimage and gaining insight from it. As such, it is similar in tone to Shirley MacLaine's treatment of the subject in *The Camino*.

Mr. Coelho tells the story of his pilgrimage within a framework tale of trying to attain to a high level of rank within an esoteric society he calls simply, "The Tradition" (in his words: "*the great fraternity that is comprised of esoteric orders from all over the world*"). Attaining this new level would result in the awarding to him of a sword. When he fails the final test, however, he is ordered by his fraternity master to perform a "redo" of the final test (penance?) by making the Santiago pilgrimage. If he succeeds, by finishing the pilgrimage and learning the lessons presented to him on the way, he'll receive his sword and rank of "Master."

Another fraternity master is assigned to guide him in the journey. His name is, Petrus (a pseudonym), and he provides instruction to Mr. Coelho along the way in the form of eleven exercises. These are recorded in the book such that the reader can try them as well.

Mr. Coelho uses the same style of very readable prose to convey the wisdom and inspiration he experienced as he used in his later book, *The Alchemist*. The big differences are the "true story" slant of this book and a

The Pilgrimage

slightly more martial tone. The latter is seen in the sword as a symbol of his desired rank and as a goal of this pilgrimage. He also refers to the idea of living life effectively as "fighting the good fight," where in *The Alchemist* he presents the same concept as "finding your Personal Legend." Both ideas work for what he is trying to say, but I prefer the latter.

Like *The Alchemist*, *The Pilgrimage* is full of quotable passages. Mr. Coelho has a knack for this and it tells me that he is a genuine seeker who has apparently had some major insights in his life. His gift is being able to share them with the world through his writing. While I think he does a better job of that in *The Alchemist*, there are some passages in *The Pilgrimage* that are golden. Such as:

Among the greatest sensations that I have experienced in my life were those I felt on that unforgettable first night on the Road to Santiago. It was cold, despite its being summer, but I could still taste the warmth of the wine that Petrus had brought. I looked up at the sky; the Milky Way spread across it, reflecting the immensity of the Road we would have to travel. This immensity made me very anxious; it created a terrible fear that I would not be able to succeed— that I was too small for this task.

The rest of the book is the account of Mr. Coelho learning to measure up, and for that, it is inspiring. Along the way, he converses with angels and demons, fights with a demon-possessed dog, and engages in an ancient Templar rite in a set of ruins in the dead of night. He presents all this as factual, and I won't dismiss it. The universe is big and I think we generally are far from understanding our place in it. At the least, as with Shirley MacLaine's book, I can take such passages as instructional parables. It is probably the spiritual nature of the Santiago Camino that prompts such accounts from its pilgrims.

Paulo Coelho's *The Pilgrimage* is a worthy addition to the body of tales of the Santiago de Compostela Camino. Its readable, personal story of an individual's journey along the ancient roadway, and through life, will inspire both the ardent traveler and the seeker of truth.

Man's Search for Meaning

Author: Viktor Frankl
Publisher: Beacon Press, Boston
Publication date: 06/01/2006
Pages: 188
ASIN: B009U9S6Fl
Type: Nonfiction, Counseling & Psychology
Ray's rating: 5 stars

The first version of this review appeared on the www.goodreads.com and www.booklikes.com websites in October of 2015.

RAY-VIEW

I HAVE run across quotes from Vicktor Frankl's *Man's Search for Meaning* for a long time now. I see it referred to very often, usually in the context of considering a hopeless situation (i.e., many world events). Reviewers often refer to it as "life changing" and it remains one of the most popular books of all time.

So I finally got my own copy and I was greatly impressed. I'm not a big fan of modern psychology that sees people as no more than "brain containers," but Dr. Frankl saw (he died in 1997) beyond that, and his credentials were experiential and not just academic.

Dr. Frankl was a psychologist in Austria in the 1930s when the Nazis invaded. Though he had an American immigration visa and could have escaped, he chose to remain with his aged parents and so was arrested with them and the rest of his family. He then spent three years in concentration camps, mostly Auschwitz, until he was liberated by the advancing American army. His entire family (including his pregnant wife) died in the camps.

When Dr. Frankl was arrested (for being Jewish) he hung onto a manuscript he had been working on that was about logotherapy--a slant on psychology that he was the principal developer of (though others apparently contributed to its antecedents). Producing this book was his passionate project and he tried to keep the manuscript even though he knew it was hopeless in the face of prisoners having absolutely everything taken from them. He lost the manuscript, but not his desire for creating the book.

Man's Search for Meaning

In a nutshell, he found the strength to endure the unimaginable horrors of the concentration camps from his sense of living for something more than himself. This sense included his desire to reunite with his wife (he didn't know until after the war that she had died soon after arriving at Auschwitz) and his desire to write his book. Of course, he didn't know that this was what was saving him until he evaluated his experiences afterwards, and his insights became *Man's Search for Meaning* (which was published under different titles for different editions).

Dr. Frankl's insights gleaned from his time in the camps are the great allure of this book. What he discovered about the meaning of life in the face of extreme oppression offers hope and guidance for anyone trying to cope with the more common, day-to-day, oppressions. That hope comes from people finding a meaning to their lives, and Dr. Frankl tells us that it can be found in three ways:

(1) by creating a work or doing a deed; (2) by experiencing something or encountering someone; and (3) by the attitude we take toward unavoidable suffering.

This indicates why pilgrimages can be such powerful bringers of insight. The thing to note about these three ways is their external nature. That is, they are a response to outside stimuli even if that stimuli is deliberately engaged (such as deciding to hike the Santiago de Compostela Camino). This leads to a central tenet of Dr. Frankl's:

Don't aim at success— the more you aim at it and make it a target, the more you are going to miss it.

I can amen that in my life many times over. It's basically "trying too hard" and can even be compounded by hubris. Dr. Frankl goes on to emphasize this point:

The more one forgets himself— by giving himself to a cause to serve or another person to love— the more human he is and the more he actualizes himself.

When people don't have something or someone to live for, they can come to a point of questioning what they are indeed living for. "What's the use?" is the question they want to answer but can't. Dr. Frankl calls this state an "existential vacuum." He says:

The existential vacuum manifests itself mainly in a state of boredom.

Ray-views

Another big "amen." This can be a big problem for workers and leads, in my experience, to job burnout. Dr. Frankl does not miss this and examines it in the light of people who have lost their jobs. The depression that results for them he calls, "unemployment neurosis." He says:

...being jobless was equated with being useless, and being useless was equated with having a meaningless life.

I was most interested in this existential vacuum that grips the prisoner and the corporate worker in similar fashion. I think a useful study might be made in comparing the psychology of the concentration camp inmate and the modern corporate worker. Based on the insights of this book, I would say they share a common crisis and a common solution.

Dr. Frankl avers the solution lies outside the self. Meaning, he says, comes from the world (universe) and is not imposed upon it. It is the individual's responsibility to find that someone and/or something that to them is worth living for, and that is transcendent of everything else. Achieving this insight, will allow them to endure suffering when it comes.

There are so many insights to take away from this book! Most thoughtful people will find something in it that speaks to them. *Man's Search for Meaning* is not a long book, but is one to be savored, over and over, and digested. It goes a long way towards making sense of the world as we experience it, and offering insight to deal with it, more than most books I've read. It deserves its place as a world classic in self-help and psychology literature.

By his own account, Dr. Frankl survived the death camps through a lot of luck and fortunate (for him) choices made by those around him. I like to think it was a benign force for good that preserved his insights in the face of the most oppressive of evils for the sake of us, in this age, who so desperately need it.

Run

Author: Ann Patchett
Publisher: HarperCollins Publishers
Publication date: 7/29/2008
Pages: 320
ISBN-13: 9780061340642
Type: Fiction, American, Contemporary
Ray's rating: 3 stars
Characters: Bernadette, Doyle, Sullivan, Teddy Hall, Tennessee, Kenya, Tip

The first version of this review appeared on the www.goodreads.com and www.booklikes.com websites in October of 2013.

RAY-VIEW

I THINK, mostly, *Run* is a book about family. Not family based on blood ties, the Doyles are largely a family created through adoption, but rather, family as created by love ties. That's what makes it compelling and why I stuck with it to the end. Of course, Ann Patchett is an excellent writer and her prose is easy to follow, so reading her is never a chore. But this "literary" story is not the kind I would ordinarily pick up except that I liked her earlier novel, *Bel Canto*.

The story of *Run* centers around an Irish-Catholic family that struggles with the death of their beloved mother, the strains of parental expectations versus individual desires, being an interracial Catholic family, sacrificing for love of family, and performing well also for the love of family.

The story opens with the death of the mother, Bernadette, who had been adored by her husband, their one biological child, and the two young black sons they had adopted as infants. But there is a conflict in the extended families--the Doyles and the Sullivans--over who should get the family heirloom. This is a statute of the Virgin Mary that bears a remarkable resemblance to Bernadette. The family tradition is that the statue should pass to the daughter that looks most like it, but the Doyles had no daughters and only one biological son. The father, simply referred to as "Doyle," puts off the decision, preferring to keep the statue for the comfort of the adopted boys until they are grown and the decision is forced.

Ray-views

The statue conflict isn't resolved until the end of the novel. For the most of the book, the story moves ahead to the time when the boys, Tip and Teddy, are much older. Tip is at Harvard studying fish (his passion) and Teddy is in High School. Doyle, a former mayor of Boston, tries to ingrain a civic awareness in the boys and he desires that they get into politics as he did. They don't share his political enthusiasm, however. Tip only wants to be an ichthyologist and Teddy's only passion is to be a faithful Catholic, and maybe even become a priest. The oldest son, Sullivan, left years ago to do charitable work in Africa because he couldn't fulfill his father's desires for him. He was also estranged because his father channeled his affections to his adopted sons when Sullivan disappointed him.

Against this background, the plot (such as it is) takes off when one night, after hearing a lecture by Jesse Jackson, Tip is arguing with Doyle and doesn't see an SUV bearing down on him in the midst of a heavy snowfall. He is saved by a black woman who appears out of nowhere and pushes him out of the vehicle's path, only to be struck herself. Tip and the woman stranger are taken to the hospital. He suffers a broken ankle, but she has a broken hip and other injuries. The woman's eleven year-old daughter was with her and the Doyles take her into their care. The woman turns out to be Tip and Teddy's biological mother, who has been watching their development from afar all these years. Her daughter, Kenya, is aware of her relationship to the boys and has idolized them and their adopting family herself.

The development of the relationships between these characters makes up the story. This is decidedly a character-driven, rather than plot-driven, novel. The characters are sympathetic, each with their own passions, angers, and faults. There are no "bad guys" here. Conflicts stem from differing agendas and needs. Tension is built from the process of their working it all out. Ms Patchett is skillful in this and draws the reader into the process, so you come to care for these people and to pull for them.

I liked the book, but had the feeling I had heard it before. Hasn't the story of an open-minded white couple raising brilliant black children been done a few times? It might have been more ground-breaking to have an open-minded black couple raising brilliant white kids (or maybe average, bratty white kids). It struck me the kids were too brilliant, and too good. And the oldest, Sullivan, was too forgiving somehow. I think the idea was for a reconciliation that brings him back into the family. It's a beautiful thought, but I think it needed a little more development. As it is, the reconciliation was too sudden and stretched credulity.

Run

But still, I liked these characters. Even Teddy, though his reciting lengthy quotes from famous people was more annoying than impressive. I liked Tip's scholarly introversion and his conflict between desire and duty. I liked Sullivan's outgoing compassion and Kenya's innocent support of everyone. Even Doyle's good intentions with not-so-good consequences earn him sympathy for trying. Seeing all these reconcile and make a family was the best part of this story for me.

I'm not clear on why the book is entitled, *Run*. There's the obvious allusions to Doyle's political leanings and his desire for his boys to run for office, and to Kenya's love of running track. It may have something to do with running (for office) being what the boys don't want to do, and with running track being what Kenya wants to do. Or Sullivan running away from his father may play into it. Maybe everybody is just running in one way or another.

Ms Patchett did do a good job at setting her scenes. She provides a good feel for the Boston area, the effects of a heavy northeastern snow, and the ambiance of Catholicism. Overall, though I liked the characters and the writing, I felt the story was a bit too stereotyped and light on drama. I rated it 3 stars because I know Ms Patchett can do better.

State of Wonder

Author: Ann Patchett
Publisher: HarperCollins Publishers
Publication date: 5/8/2012
Pages: 384
ISBN-13: 9780062049810
Type: Fiction, Contemporary, Literary
Ray's rating: 4 stars
Characters: Marina Singh, Dr. Annick Swenson, Anders Eckman, Easter, Jim Fox, Barbara Bovender

The first version of this review appeared on the www.goodreads.com website in November of 2013.

RAY-VIEW

STATE OF WONDER is a character-driven, imaginative, inspirational story and in my opinion, Ann Patchett's best to-date. Set mostly in the Amazon jungle, it does evoke the emotion of that exotic place but in a grounded, gritty, realistic way. It is nuanced with many levels and I expect readers will find one suitable for their attachment. At the highest level, I would say it is the story of a person who represents a very current, scientific and clinical outlook who discovers the wonder outside of her box, and brings it home.

The protagonist in *State of Wonder* is Dr. Marina Singh, who works for Vogel, a pharmaceutical company. She is sent to the Amazon jungle to investigate the death of a colleague there and also to determine the status of the work being done by another company doctor, Dr. Swenson, on a drug that prolongs the time of fertility for women. She finds Brazil a different world from her Minnesota home, though there are at least some points of similarity in the city of Manaus. The city is on the edge of the jungle and it barely clings to western civilization through deliberate artifices like the opera house. There, Dr. Singh finds her connection to the familiar before heading down the Rio Negro and into the jungle.

This boat ride is the start of Dr. Singh's immersion into the jungle, which teems with wild life that she must cope with constantly. Insects, especially, are an omnipresence and Ms Patchett shows that with wonderful passages like this:

State of Wonder

At dusk the insects came down in a storm: the hard-shelled and soft-sided, the biting and stinging, the chirping and buzzing and droning, every last one unfolded its paper wings and flew with unimaginable velocity into the eyes and mouths and noses of the only three humans they could find.

There's no escape from the annoyances of such ubiquitous creatures just as there is no escape from the hard parts of our lives. But we can see beyond that, to the greater wonder. As Dr. Swenson says to Dr. Singh a few paragraphs later:

In an instant the veil of insects lifted and Marina saw nothing as she had never seen nothing before. It was as if God Himself had turned out the lights, every last one, and left them in the gaping darkness of His abandonment.

"Open your eyes, Dr Singh," Dr. Swenson said. "Look at the stars."

She did not know enough numbers to count them, and even if she did, the stars could not be separated one from the other, the whole was so much greater than the sum of its parts.

I think beholding that whole *is* the state of wonder. Ms Patchett fills her book with such nuggets.

I believe Ms Patchett's writing forte is her depiction of characters who are interesting and believable. We are drawn into their plights and ventures, even the secondary characters, and we follow their tales with relish and find they are just as interesting as the plot threads.

And there is a definite plot to *State of Wonder* that we are compelled to follow to the end. I don't do spoilers in reviews, so I'll just say that Dr. Singh finds Dr. Swenson and discovers her fertility drug work is based on the proclivity of the local Lakashi women to conceive well into advanced age. The source of that proclivity is the bark of a local tree, which is also helpful beyond matters of female fertility. Singh discovers the fate of her colleague, Dr. Eckman, and in the process does battle with a giant anaconda and faces mortal danger from a tribe of cannibals. Her escape requires an impossible decision and great sacrifice.

While Ms Patchett does provide some basic jungle adventure, she tempers it with some insightful humor, as when Dr. Singh is mistaken for a local and must "perform" for the tourists with them. She endures a little humiliation out of respect for the indigenous people.

There are some neat plot twists and a big one towards the end that I didn't see coming, though I guess I should have. Ms Patchett handles it

Ray-views

masterfully. It all leads to a very satisfying ending that will keep you musing over this story for a long time. But there are some definite, unresolved story threads that could easily plot a sequel. Of course, it may be Ms Patchett's intention to say that much in life is left unresolved. While that's true, I do hope she carries this story and its characters a little further.

There is a character, Dr. Rapp, who has died by the time of the story events but whose life and actions setup the situation that begins *State of Wonder*. He is fondly remembered by Dr. Swenson and is held as the example of a person who has achieved the wondrous state:

He was fully engaged with his life every minute that he lived it. He didn't trudge along doing what someone else told him to do. He was never a cog in the wheel. He held up his head and looked at the world around him.

Awareness without distraction may be the secret to a life well-lived and to finding the wonder in life. That wonder, being all around us, requires of a person only to truly open their eyes. The idea of opening your awareness is repeated through the story, and best so in the quote most often noted in reviews:

Never be so focused on what you're looking for that you overlook the thing you actually find.

To do so is to really see all that is around you and achieve that state of wonder. Ms Patchett shows us in her wonderful story that it's a good state to reach.

Wild: From Lost to Found on the Pacific Crest Trail

Author: Cheryl Strayed
Publisher: Knopf Doubleday Publishing Group
Publication date: 11/18/2014
Pages: 336
ISBN-13: 9781101873441
Type: Nonfiction, Travel, Adventure
Ray's rating: 5 stars
Characters: Cheryl Strayed (author)

The first version of this review appeared on the www.amazon.com, www.goodreads.com, and www.booklikes.com websites in June of 2015.

RAY-VIEW

WILD is author Cheryl Strayed's memoir about her three-month long hike up the Pacific Crest Trail (PCT) in 1995. Only 26 years old at the time, she walked the trail alone. Though she had done a good bit of camping in her youth, she was not a backpacker. Her motivation was the classic seeker's quest for self-discovery and insight after her world had been shattered by the death of her mother four years prior. They had been very close and when she lost that relationship, she found she couldn't function in a normal life. Her remaining family--brother, sister, stepfather--drifted apart without her mother there as a binding agent. She couldn't function as a wife either, and, shortly before her personal pilgrimage, she divorced.

She was lost and desperate for an answer--not so much an answer as to why her life fell apart, as much as how to put it back together. That she would seek her answer through an eleven hundred mile hike came through serendipity. She found a PCT hiker's guide in a sporting goods store and was drawn to it. Eventually, she bought it and acted on it.

In describing the lost emptiness she was feeling after her mother's death, Ms Strayed says:

It took me years to take my place among the ten thousand things again...I would suffer. I would suffer. I would want things to be different than they were. The wanting

Ray-views

was a wilderness and I had to find my own way out of the woods. It took me four years, seven months, and three days to do it. I didn't know where I was going until I got there.

In short, she decided to look for the way out of her emotional wilderness by navigating a real one. By living the metaphor, and then writing about it, Cheryl Strayed takes her place among those pilgrims who make sacred journeys such as the Santiago de Compostela Camino. Many share their insights with us, and Ms Strayed does so with considerable literary skills.

Wild is written as creative nonfiction and so reads like a novel with a first-person point-of-view. The prose is solid, intelligent, honest, and a delight to read. Ms Strayed's "story" construction is also solid and balanced so well between narrative, flashbacks, and insightful exposition, that the reader is as engrossed as with any thriller. I think that's owing to the author's writing abilities and her literary passion. She says:

Of all the things I'd done in my life, of all the versions of myself I'd lived out, there was one that had never changed: I was a writer.

She certainly is and that could make a reader wonder as to how much of her story is fictionalized. I suspect, not much, and probably much less than Paulo Coelho's *The Pilgrimage*. But truth is not always revealed in a simple recitation of facts. More is to be found in the experiencer's interpretation and that is the joy of this book. It is engrossing because the author is dealing with problems and emotions that are common to most of us, and so it's easy to relate to the hints at answers she finds. She gives us those hints in many beautiful passages that show the metaphor in the things she saw on her journey. Such as:

This was once a wasteland of lava and pumice and ash. This was once an empty bowl that took hundreds of years to fill. But hard as I tried, I couldn't see them in my mind's eye. Not the mountain or the wasteland or the empty bowl. They simply were not there anymore. There was only the stillness and silence of that water: what a mountain and a wasteland and an empty bowl turned into after the healing began.

When you get to that passage, you can readily see that she is talking about herself as much as she is describing Crater Lake.

But *Wild* is not just a book of beautiful prose and spiritual insights, it is a memoir that deals with the get-down grittiness of life. Ms Strayed is brutally honest in relating her life for that time period. She speaks forthrightly of her flirtations with heroin and her seeking solace in sexual

Wild

encounters. Those were other wildernesses she had to find her way out of, and I expect many of her readers will relate. That she did find her way out, and came to terms with herself, is expressed in another insightful passage:

What if I forgave myself? I thought. What if I forgave myself even though I'd done something I shouldn't have?...What if I was sorry, but if I could go back in time I wouldn't do anything differently than I had done?...What if heroin taught me something? What if 'yes' was the right answer instead of 'no?' What if what made me do all those things everyone thought I shouldn't have done was what also had got me here? What if I was never redeemed? What if I already was?

  Wild strikes me as a seeker's attempt to reach the bones of life's meaning. In that regard, it is a descendant of Thoreau's *Walden*. In such a work, you won't find definitive answers or endorsements of anybody's dogmas. But in looking at the collective of such works, you'll find a literature filled with a searching spirit that is simply asking the question: "What the Hell is this all about?" If there is an answer, it is a dynamic one, found in the continual asking of the question.

  By the time you've read the last page of *Wild*, you won't have found a statement of Ms Strayed's "answer." There is no final "moral of the story" that you can print out and frame and hang on the wall. You will find a lot of statements throughout the book that could help you find your own way (and many are worth framing). In the end, though, Ms Strayed didn't so much find an answer, as she found a place--in the world and in her heart--where she could dwell with a sense of absolution. That was her salvation found on the Pacific Crest Trail.

  Such is the value of pilgrimages.

2001: A Space Odyssey

Author: Arthur C. Clarke
Publisher: Arthur C. Clarke and Polaris Productions, Inc.
Publication date: 2012 by RosettaBooks (first published in 1968)
Pages: 297
ISBN-13: 9780795330711
Type: Science Fiction
Ray's rating: 4 stars
Characters: Heywood Floyd, HAL 9000, Dave Bowman, Frank Poole

The first version of this review appeared on the www.amazon.com, www.goodreads.com, and www.booklikes.com websites in October of 2015.

RAY-VIEW

I SAW the movie, *2001: A Space Odyssey*, in 1968 when I was 12 years old. It was as incomprehensible to me as a child, as it was to most adults then. Even so, it was soon considered a classic science fiction film and I have spent most of my life not really understanding why. I had heard that the book was much better, but I never got around to reading it until recently. It is, indeed, much better and I think there are several reasons why.

For one thing, the novel was written by Arthur C. Clarke, one of the best SF writers ever. But even so, this novel was written under special circumstances because the story was meant to be a movie from the start--a collaboration between Mr. Clarke and film producer Stanley Kubrick. That collaboration is described by Mr. Clarke in his Foreword to the edition of the novel that I read. He says Mr. Kubrick suggested they start with a novel from which they would derive the screenplay because "...a screenplay has to specify everything in excruciating detail, [and] it is almost as tedious to read as to write."

This is more or less the way it worked out, though toward the end novel and screenplay were being written simultaneously, with feedback in both directions.

That dynamic shows in the book. Though the narrative is engaging, owing to Mr. Clarke's skills, there are sections that seem to be explanatory for the sake of the film. Some of these take the point-of-view of the aliens

2001: A Space Odyssey

in general--not of a particular alien character (e.g., chapter 37: "Experiment"). At one point, the narrative even takes the POV of the big monolith Bowman finds on Japetus. And then there are sections that are descriptions of various views in space of suns and moons and planets. They are well-done and scientifically informed, but with only a scant connection to the plot or a character. All these sections seem to be for informing the film producers and for the sake of writing the screenplay. They are informative for the novel reader because they fill in the holes left by the film's ambiguous images, but they lessen the novel's storytelling. They don't lessen it by much, though, mostly because Mr. Clarke was the author.

So the book answers questions raised by the movie. For instance, it makes clear that the monoliths were tools used by ancient and god-like aliens to influence the evolution of other life-forms. Used on our non-human ancestors of three million years ago, it exerted only a small nudge to launch them on the path to the tool-making that promoted the explosion of their intelligence. Understanding that, makes sense of the film's initial scenes of the ape-men and that image of the tossed bone morphing into the space shuttle.

We also better understand why the mission to Jupiter (actually, Saturn in the book) was undertaken. I don't recall whether the movie made it clear that the monolith found on Earth's moon sent a high-powered electromagnetic signal to Jupiter (in the book, it went to Saturn's moon, Japetus) and so prompted the human journey there. It *is* clear in the book. And the book does contain the sudden shift in narrative from the monolith's signal blasting out into space, to the spaceship, *Discovery*, as it passes through the asteroid belt. In the book as in the movie, this struck me as too sudden a shift, leaving out a needed bridge. It drops, too suddenly, the POV of Heywood Floyd, whom we had been following since the three million year scene-shift from the group of ape-men. It just doesn't feel right.

Actually, the book does offer a bit of a bridge with chapter Fourteen. There, we see, from the POV of several deep space probes, the flight of the monolith's signal across the solar system. Even an unnamed human at the Goddard Space Center is noted as picking up the signal from the various probes. Then Mr. Clarke sums up the technical observation and dramatic turning point with some smooth, descriptive prose:

> *...it was as clear and unmistakable as a vapor trail across a cloudless sky, or a single line of footprints over a field of virgin snow. Some immaterial pattern of energy,*

Ray-views

throwing off a spray of radiation like the wake of a racing speedboat, had leaped from the face of the Moon, and was heading out toward the stars.

The part about the "mutiny" of the HAL 9000 computer in the book is pretty much in sync with what was presented in the movie. The book didn't contain the "lip reading" scene, though, which was a neat part of the movie. And then HAL's murder of the hibernating crew and attempted murder of Bowman are handled a bit differently, but retain Bowman's surviving for a few minutes in a vacuum without his helmet, and his "lobotomy" of HAL.

The last part of the story, though, is where the book is way easier to follow than the film. This concerns Bowman's investigation of the big monolith he finds on the Saturn moon of Japetus and his subsequent capture by it, transport across the galaxy (the monolith is a "star gate"), and finally his transformation into the "Star-Child."

The book makes all this clearer, mostly because we have Bowman's inner monologue about what's happening to him supported by Mr. Clarke's prose exposition. This part contains a lot of those sections where I think Mr. Clarke was explaining things for the sake of the producers, but it still captures the extreme bizarreness of Bowman's evolution/transformation. The reader understands that it is being deliberately done by the aliens. In the movie, that's far less clear. The book notes that Bowman is quickly aware that the "hotel room" he lands in is an artificial construct. He finds proof by examining the objects in the room and from watching the television mounted in the ceiling over the bed. I think the movie would have worked better here for the audience if Mr. Kubrick had incorporated those points.

Finally, because the reader knows that Bowman has been transformed, via some speeded-up process of evolution, into the Star-Child, the final scene is much less enigmatic. We know that the Star-Child is David Bowman. He has been empowered by being freed from his corporeal body to become a being of energy and taking the form of the Star-Child. He begins to exercise his new power and freedoms and finds he can move across the galaxy at the speed of thought, and so returns to Earth.

All this is depicted in the movie, but not explained. I don't know how many viewers were astute enough to follow that thread.

Now Mr. Kubrick decided to leave his viewers with an artistic image of the Star-Child contemplating Earth. Most viewers were just left in confusion. Mr. Clarke's novel presents a less mysterious ending by keeping the POV with Bowman as the Star-Child and having him save

2001: A Space Odyssey

the earth from nuclear destruction. And he does this in a final chapter that is less than a page in length, and that I think is a much more satisfying ending than the movie's.

Overall, I very much enjoyed reading the novel version of *2001: A Space Odyssey*. I consider it a better presentation of the story. It contains all the enthusiasm for space age technology that was in the air in the 1960s as a result of all the PR for the "race to the moon." The imagination of that generation was captured by the possibilities of rocket and computer sciences for enabling space travel and manned missions to the planets. Mr. Clarke's writing reflects that enthusiasm for technology and is amazingly accurate in his extrapolation of it into the future. For instance, he notes the use of personal computers at a time when computers filled rooms. This passage sounds like Dr. Floyd is using an iPad:

> *When he tired of official reports and memoranda and minutes, he would plug his foolscap-size Newspad into the ship's information circuit and scan the latest reports from Earth.*

In this novel, Mr. Clarke not only makes accurate "predictions" as to future technology, but he expresses his love for it, and for its potential of providing humankind a better future. I remember this attitude and it had captured me in my youth, along with the heady desire for humankind's "leap into space." It is a hopeful attitude of the sort that made *Star Trek* a modern myth and that made Carl Sagan's books popular. Today, it has been frustrated by the US "retreat from space" and the convergence of various calamities, but I think maybe it survives in the current escape into video games. But back then, many good people believed in this mythos of space travel and sought careers in technology to be a part of it. Writers wrote about it, as Mr. Clarke does in this book with passages such as:

> *When Earth was tamed and tranquil, and perhaps a little tired, there would still be scope for those who loved freedom, for the tough pioneers, the restless adventurers. But their tools would not be ax and gun and canoe and wagon; they would be nuclear power plant and plasma drive and hydroponic farm. The time was fast approaching when Earth, like all mothers, must say farewell to her children.*

This was the belief and the hope that is all but squashed now by a space agency that is absorbed by a military pushing for constant war rather than space exploration. And it is apparent that Earth will be more than just tamed, she'll be pillaged and raped. And if any humans make it beyond

Ray-views

Earth orbit now, they'll likely be soldiers bent on conquest and exploitation, rather than "tough pioneers" or "restless adventurers."

It is conceivable that the state of real-world technology in 2001 could have approximated what Mr. Clarke and Mr. Kubrick foresaw in their story, but the urge to make profits and subdue and rule the earth took precedence over space exploration. Consequently, there appears little hope for real space odysseys anytime soon. Even if an alien artifact such as the monolith were found, I suspect our rulers' would only be concerned with how to exploit it for profit, or how to militarize it.

Still, I understand now why *2001: A Space Odyssey* is considered a classic movie, though I think it takes reading the associated novel to reach that understanding. The novel is a reminder for me of the heady days of the "space age" and the "moon race." I had all but forgotten them in these darker times. It may be that pointing out the gap between human dreams of a bold future, and the reality imposed by rulers motivated only by greed and personal power, is the greatest value of this novel. Sometimes truth-in-fiction comes indirectly.

Another Dreamer

Source: Ray's Journal, www.rayfoy.com, 02-Aug-2014

Another dreamer...He doesn't have enough money to travel. (Paulo Coelho)

THIS is how Santiago, the protagonist of Paulo Coelho's little book, *The Alchemist*, is written off by a ticket agent when he inquires about passage to Africa but doesn't follow through with a purchase. This bit of the story is significant to me in a couple of aspects. First, it equates travel with the idea of being free and living fully. Escape through travel is a common dream for people and the ticket agent recognizes that. He sees it all the time in the eyes of his customers, and with regards to Santiago, he is right. The boy is seeking a treasure by following his "Personal Legend" which is leading him to Africa. He is hitting a big wall in simply not having money for a ticket.

That brings me to the second aspect, which is capitalistic crassness--that commercial precept that commodifies everything, including dreams of freedom. It says that desire and a brave heart are not enough to pursue your life goals. You have to have money so you can make somebody else rich in the process.

I have wrestled with this problem in my life. I've had the desire to travel but not the means, and usually not the courage. At the heart of this desire are the ideas of freedom and of finding meaning in this life. Both ideas include a fair amount of subjectivity, I suppose, but I agree with Joseph Campbell who said that what the seeker is really seeking is "an experience of being alive."

...so that our life experiences on the purely physical plane will have resonance within our innermost being and reality, so that we can actually feel the rapture of being alive. (Joseph Campbell)

Our desire for that rapturous experience is what creates our mid-life crises and our feelings of diminution. We write our bucket lists and dream of breaking the chains that prevent their fulfillments. We sit in our cubicles and count a million widgets for the millionth time. A fear rises in us that we dare not voice, yet we must voice if we are to be true to ourselves. And if we can do so, we speak in agreement with Eowyn in *The Return of the King*, who, when asked what it is she fears, replies:

A cage," [Éowyn] said. "To stay behind bars, until use and old age accept them, and all chance of doing great deeds is gone beyond recall or desire. (Tolkien)

To lose the desire is the saddest part.

I believe we go on when we are done with this life, but that doesn't mitigate the disappointment of having wasted it. So we live with the aching need to give vent to a primal scream and run from our cubicles and out the corporate doors. Only then can we go to a distant land and stand on a mountain and gaze upon a sacred valley. There, in the cool morning air, we will feel the energy reaching out to us from the earth, from past lives and companion spirits. This is the point we want to reach; a beginning from which we would live the remainder of our life in earnest, squeezing from it every morsel of being and inspiration until we can see it plainly in front of us, and know it for what it is.

When we find our cages strong and our bucket list goals unreachable, we often turn to stories--books and movies (even video games)--to provide that inspiration we can't experience in the living world. Some stories do a good job of describing our cage and portraying our escape. Ben Stiller really brought this out in his movie, *The Secret Life of Walter Mitty*. In Stiller's version of Thurber's story, Mitty spends his life in a basement workspace where he has been "doing his job" for years, suppressing his impulse to experience life, and venting through lucid imaginings until he finally chooses to take a step into reality. That step leads him to some extensive traveling that allows him to experience the wider world, and so find the reality of his own being.

In Stiller's movie and in Coelho's book, travel is used as a symbol of living deliberately and fully in the moment. To achieve such living--the experience of being alive--is the reason for breaking free in the first place. In both stories, that breaking free is begun with a decision. Santiago decides to explore his Personal Legend, and Walter Mitty decides to search for the photo-journalist himself rather than let someone else do it. So the step into the wider world begins with the simple decision to do so.

But there may be obstacles to overcome in carrying out that first step--maybe really big ones. For Santiago, it was simply that he had no money (i.e., the means), hence, the ticket seller's comment. Walter Mitty had to overcome his deep rut and his lack of belief in himself. Such

Another Dreamer

obstacles are often the manifestations of practiced, internal inertia that we may hear as a voice inside.

The Miley Cyrus song, "The Climb," (by Jessi Alexander and Jon Mabe) begins with the words:

I can almost see it,
That dream I am dreaming,
But there's a voice inside my head saying
"You'll never reach it"

I hear that voice every day. It is the accuser, berating me for being so foolish as to think I have any hope of breaking out of my cage. It tells me the world is too small, and the evil in it is too great. It says I'm lucky to be surviving, that my novel will suck, and that I'm not even a good and faithful servant. It tells me I don't have the money to travel, and that even if I did, all I would see is a tourist's veneer in front of a wasted, dying world.

But I keep trying. Something won't let me give up. For some reason, I keep believing I will find a way to fly out of my cage. I think this is not courage so much as not being able (or willing) to do anything else. It may be a *Don Quixote* kind of courage, where I follow a dream in the face of a reality that pummels me, sometimes greatly. Such "courage" is often called naiveté or lunacy, and is usually ridiculed; then it becomes a matter of sheer endurance.

So endure, my friend, and know that the pursuit of your passion, your Personal Legend, is enhanced many-fold when it includes helping others. Especially if your help contributes towards their finding their Personal Legends. I hope this helps you find yours.

As for me, I still want someday to stand on a mountain and view a sacred valley. I want to feel that rapture of being alive because I am NOT a good and faithful servant.

I'm just another dreamer.

Moving vs Traveling
(Reflections on *Life of Pi*)

Source: Ray's Journal, www.rayfoy.com, 06-Sep-2014; (All quotes are from Yann Martel's *Life of Pi*).

I RECENTLY finished reading Yann Martel's book, *Life of Pi*. I had heard of it, because of the movie version, but I had not seen the movie and really wasn't sure what it was about. From the movie previews I thought it was something about a young man lost at sea on a lifeboat with a tiger. That's an interesting twist on the basic ocean survival story, but it never struck me as compelling enough to see the movie or investigate the book. I understood that the book was doing well internationally and the movie was so-so, and I left it at that.

Then, recently, my wife read the book and was enthralled with it. So I read it upon her recommendation and became enthralled myself. Yes, the story action is mostly of a teenaged Indian boy who survives a ship sinking only to end up on a lifeboat with an adult Bengal tiger. Just that aspect of the book is engrossing and makes it a page-turner, but overall, the story is about religion. It is an extended parable that speaks to how our religions are stories that we embrace to help us get through life. That's all I'll say about that here. For this journal entry, I want to reflect on some of the themes and points Mr. Martel makes in his book.

Life of Pi was one of those works that spoke to me on many different levels. There was much that I related to and "amened" as I read, and I discovered even more as I wrote my Ray-view. For example, he makes a really good point about moving.

I've made a number of moves with my family. I mean physical moves--packing up our stuff and moving to another city or part of the same city. A number of them involved house purchases. Why did we do this? If asked that question at those times I would have replied something about going to a better job opportunity, school district, compatible environment, or some such. But Mr. Martel stated my reasons very accurately:

Moving vs Traveling (Reflections on *Life of Pi*)

People move because of the wear and tear of anxiety. Because of the gnawing feeling that no matter how hard they work their efforts will yield nothing, that what they build up in one year will be torn down in one day by others. Because of the impression that the future is blocked up, that they might do all right but not their children. Because of the feeling that nothing will change, that happiness and prosperity are possible only somewhere else.

Yes, that's exactly why we moved when we moved. And there was good and bad with each move. In none of them did we find that place that was "just right" for us. We ended up coming back to our home city, but then moved around a lot within it. I think we have lived in its every major section and found, once again, that there were good and bad aspects to all of them. All-in-all, we did manage to provide decent places for our kids to grow up, but we never found that the move was the answer. The "wear and tear of anxiety" always caught up with us. We found that happiness and prosperity were conditions we had to create for ourselves, wherever we happen to be (though "prosperity" is a matter of definition). I think we've stopped looking for that in a place. If we move again, it will be with different motivations.

Now I must make a distinction between moving and traveling. *Moving* from one residence to another has been, for me, an act of trying to *find* something, as Mr. Martel stated so well. *Traveling*, has been an act of trying to *experience* something. In the little of it I've done, it has always been a seeking for what Joseph Campbell says is that "rapture of being alive." I have made the seeking of that rapture my quest, whether actually doing it or just dreaming about it.

Travel, as an idea and experience, is a classic metaphor and symbol for life lived fully. It is used that way in Ben Stiller's *Walter Mitty* movie, and it was what moved me so much when a celebrity visited my city who was known for his travels.

And yet, though travel is widely conceived as a means to "broaden the mind," that broadening can also occur when much spiritual or emotional distance is covered rather than physical miles. Such inner traveling can take us to a new perspective. Indeed, it can be so new that treading our worn paths is like breaking new ground. We see, for the first time, what has always been there, but overlooked. This occurred for Mr. Martel's hero, Pi, when taking a familiar way home after a visit that included a spiritual inspiration:

Ray-views

...I suddenly felt I was in heaven. The spot was in fact no different from when I had passed it not long before, but my way of seeing it had changed. The feeling, a paradoxical mix of pulsing energy and profound peace, was intense and blissful...I knelt a mortal; I rose an immortal. I felt like the centre of a small circle coinciding with the centre of a much larger one.

I think our being becomes lighter at such times. We live then at a higher frequency and concentration. These are the only times in our lives that we remember with clarity, and so we are motivated to strive for them. This is the quest of the holy and the wise, each approaching from their preferred direction.

Moving might be necessary and even a positive, but traveling is usually better, especially if it's done out of a desire for experience. In either case, the distance covered is best measured within.

The Secret Life of Walter Mitty

Source: Ray's Journal, www.rayfoy.com, 01-Jan-2014

UNREALIZED potential may be the hardest thing for a person to face in this life. If, as the Buddhists say, the root of life's sorrow is its impermanence, then reaching one's later years with no feeling of accomplishment can bring a profound sadness. It is an unstamped passport, an empty travel journal, or a backpack never used.

All of those images are in Ben Stiller's adaptation of James Thurber's *The Secret Life of Walter Mitty*. I saw the movie recently with my family and we all enjoyed it. In fact, we saw it in a full theatre where I picked up on a positive energy from the entire audience. There were a lot of communal laughs that I haven't heard at a movie in a long time. It was like everyone was really into the story and just expressing their enjoyment without being aware of everyone else around them. I take that as a sign of a well-made movie and this one certainly was.

The character of Walter Mitty is so ingrained in popular thought that the name is a metaphor for someone who is a dreamer in the sense of "wannabe." The common expression is "Walter Mitty type" when describing someone who fantasizes about being someone else, especially a more exciting persona. The dreamer's desire is motivated by a wish to escape dull or otherwise unpleasant circumstances that he finds are imprisoning. His ability to make his escape is all but nil, so there is an element of tragedy in that fantasies are all he has. Don Quixote, on the other hand, at least acted on his dream in a concrete way, though it often earned him a beating. He was not just dreaming the impossible dream, he was attempting to live it.

I think more of us identify with Walter Mitty than with Don Quixote. We dream because that's all we can do. We don't have the means or the freedom to truly live in earnest, so we keep quiet and leave our debt-financed Land Rover (or Lexus) in the parking garage while we spend the day in our cubicle.

Ben Stiller's movie starts with this more-tragic image, showing Mitty as a photo negative processor at *Life* magazine. He's 42, works in the

Ray-views

basement, is threatened with job loss when *Life* is taken over by new management, and he can't even work up the courage to send an *e-harmony* "wink" to a coworker he has the hots for (and when he does, it doesn't go through). His *e-harmony* profile is devoid of "things done." These negatives prompt Mitty's escapist imaginings (with much high-tech embellishment) as he "zones out" in stressful situations.

But Mr. Stiller doesn't leave us with a trapped, disillusioned, Walter Mitty. For all his problems, Mitty has potential. He is smart, resourceful, imaginative, and even a skilled skateboarder. He just needs the courage and motivation to cross that line into a fulfilling life (don't we all believe that?).

This scenario is common in movies, where the bored and boring protagonist comes into his own by finding adventure, love, etc. This is the essence of "coming of age" stories (re: *Star Wars*). It can make for a predictable and sappy story, but Mr. Stiller doesn't fall into that trap. He could have, had he made Mitty's "breakout" be a mission to save the world, or to rescue the heroine from terrorists, or right some huge wrong. But Mitty doesn't need to save the world, just himself.

So Mr. Stiller doesn't send him chasing the Holy Grail. He goes looking for one of the magazine's photographers, Sean O'Connell (played by Sean Penn), as part of his search for a lost photo negative meant to be the cover for *Life*'s final print issue. His search takes him globetrotting and so he finally gets his passport stamped, fills his travel journal, and makes good use of his backpack. More important, he experiences life and stops zoning-out.

I've identified with Walter Mitty ever since I read Thurber's story in High School. I expect that's true for many people, just judging by the audience reaction at the movie. But though Walter Mitty or Don Quixote characters are enjoyed in stories, they are often condemned in life as aimless dreamers. Yet the character persists in our entertainments. I think that's because some of us realize that it's better to dream of an ideal, than live a delusion and believe it's real.

I consider *The Secret Life of Walter Mitty* to be Ben Stiller's best movie. I like that he made Mitty's redeeming activity to be travel, rather than fighting aliens or saving the president or some such. It makes Mitty's personal journey more relatable. This is underscored by the realistic feel of the travel scenes (even when dealing with sharks and volcanoes; and they're funny--I especially liked the scene with the drunken helicopter pilot).

In the movie, Mitty is prompted to step outside his "box" by his need to track down O'Connell. He is reluctant at first, because finding

The Secret Life of Walter Mitty

O'Connell will require some world travel, starting with his last known whereabouts, Greenland. Life opens up to him when Mitty takes the plunge, and I can relate, to a degree. When my wife and I were talking about a trip to Mexico, I felt the inertia of fear and self-doubt about making such a trip, but I bit the bullet and did it. I got my passport stamped for the first time. When the trip was done and we were flying back, I was ready to keep going and see other places. So, like Walter Mitty, I can find the courage to step out-of-doors, and even be taken by the wanderlust, if I can find the motivation and the material wherewithal.

And I liked that Mr. Stiller cast Shirley MacLaine in the role of Walter Mitty's mother. That casting embraces the movie's "travel broadens the mind" theme because Ms MacLaine is a restless world traveler, experiencer, and author. Those are things I would love to be as well, and I suppose many people feel the same. A few people realize these activities and compose their identities from their experience of the wider world.

The rest of us just dream.

The Way

Source: Ray's Journal, www.rayfoy.com, 07-May-2015

...since all things are new, you see only the beauty in them, and you feel happy to be alive. That's why a religious pilgrimage has always been one of the most objective ways of achieving insight.

> Coelho, Paulo (2009-10-13). *The Pilgrimage* (p. 35). HarperCollins. Kindle Edition.

I AM not Catholic, and am at best, "spiritual but not religious." Even so, I became enamored with the Santiago de Compostela Camino ever since I read Shirley MacLaine's book, *The Camino*. The idea of this spiritual pilgrimage, that is traditionally Catholic but with ancient, spiritual antecedents, captured my longing for insight into the "why" of this world. It spurred my desire to see beyond my bubble and into reality. And so *The Camino* became one of my favorite books and I developed a deep respect for Shirley MacLaine as a fellow seeker.

I also discovered Paulo Coelho from his wonderful little book, *The Alchemist*, where the author offers a tremendous parable of what life is really about and how we should live it. Then I discovered that Mr. Coelho also traveled the Camino and wrote a book about it. He called that book, *The Pilgrimage*, and it too became one of my favorites.

So what is it about this ancient path from the Pyrenees to the Atlantic Ocean across northern Spain that inspires such devotion? Is it the idea that St. James' bones are preserved at the end of the trek? That kings and popes have made the journey over the ages? Or maybe that the road follows a major leyline (a path of earth energy)? I don't know; maybe all of the above. It may be just the simple need to believe in a place and in an act that acknowledges the faith and desire of the seeker to find insight. Or maybe just the exertion of asking the question and making the quest is all that is required to open the seeker to input from a high spiritual connection. In any case, the idea of pilgrimage is compelling.

The Way

I had heard that a good movie to watch for those curious about the Camino was *The Way*, made by Emilio Estevez and starring his father, Martin Sheen. I watched it recently and added it to my list of favorite inspirational dramas.

This movie is one of 7 that are a collaboration between the father and son team. While it is not a thriller or a scifi/fantasy blockbuster epic, it is obviously a labor of love. I understand that Mr. Sheen had made the pilgrimage with his son, Taylor, and wished to express his love of the trek in a documentary. His son, Emilio (*The Breakfast Club*), however, thought the journey would be best expressed in a drama. They finally agreed on the latter and *The Way* was the result.

The story is of an American ophthalmologist (Tom Avery), a man in his sixties, who receives word of his son Daniel's death in France. Daniel has died in a storm in the Pyrenees mountains after being only one day on his journey down the Santiago de Compostela Camino (The Camino). Tom travels to France to retrieve his son's body and learns there the facts surrounding his son's quest and death. He also learns about the Camino and so makes the connection between his estranged relationship to his dead son, and his son's desire to make the pilgrimage. So he decides to make the Camino journey himself, scattering Daniel's ashes along the way.

In making this pilgrimage, Tom encounters some fellow pilgrims who become his reluctant (to him) companions. One is a Dutchman (Joost) with an appreciation of recreational drugs, a Canadian woman (Sara) who is walking to find the strength to quit smoking, and an Irish writer (Jack) who is seeking to overcome his "writer's block." Tom's challenge is to overcome his own cold veneer and learn to open up to life and to the goodwill of others.

Walking the Camino is a personal act of faith. It is one that most people, in modern society, will judge as crazy for all but the religiously fanatic (often judged as a kind of insanity). It is one of those acts that takes one outside the norm of existence and threatens to expose our inadequacies and fears. It is therefore both understandable and dangerous. This idea is expressed in the movie in an early scene of Tom's remembrance of a conversation with Daniel about his choice of life vocation (or his "non-choice"). Daniel had said to his father:

You don't choose a life, Dad. You live one.

Tom can't understand what his son is saying here. How many parents would? We want our children to be safe and cared for, so that they don't suffer in their lives. We want them to have the assurance of no

Ray-views

worries about food, shelter, clothing, and all the extras. If we wish them spiritual comfort, it is usually in the form of religious dogmas. What if they figure out for themselves that thing we are missing? They might want to walk the Camino, and place greater value on that experience than the sum of Bill Gates' checking account. Can we accept that? Understand it? If we're lucky, maybe we'll take up the quest ourselves.

It is said that walking the Camino brings about change in the pilgrim. Well, that's the intent. Shirley MacLaine says:

> *This can be disturbing and frightening because it means that through this energy one becomes a more psychic being--for better or for worse...The experience of complete surrender to God and self is the motivation behind most people's attempt at the Santiago de Compostela Camino.* (Shirley Maclaine, *The Camino*, p5, 2000 Pocket Books edition)

Perhaps the value of the Camino and other pilgrimages is that challenge to our bodies and spirits that the pilgrim is forced to struggle with. The struggle will take up the motivations the pilgrim brought with him and reveal the truth or delusion in them, and that will be the journey's lesson to the receptive soul.

The Way is a quiet expression of faith. Not in the religious sense, but in a deeper, spiritual one that affirms universal good and its power of transformation. The central character, Tom, has grown to middle-age, closed off from love of family and friends by a shell hardened over time. The breaking of that shell is the Camino's lesson for him that leaves him a better person.

Finding out who we are, and the power we have, is the primary value of pilgrimages. Here's to seeking yours.

Ultreya!

Suggested for Further Reading

How the Irish Saved Civilization by Thomas Cahill

Eight Mindful Steps to Happiness by Bhante Henepola Gunaratana

The Lord of the Rings (trilogy) by J.R.R. Tolkien

Gulliver's Travels by Jonathan Swift

Don Quixote by Miguel de Cervantes

The Secret Life of Walter Mitty by James Thurber

Ray-views

Storytelling

YES, this is my "catch all" category. It is Ray-views of books that don't fit easily into any of the other categories, but that still touched me with good storytelling or were otherwise meaningful to me.

I'm fascinated with the writing process and storytelling, fiction or not. I am an artist at heart and my heroes are artists--Da Vinci, Michelangelo, Shakespeare, Tolkien, Suzanne Collins, Paulo Coelho, Daniel Quinn, Ann Patchett, David Mitchell, Viktor Frankl, and many others. These are people able to express their vision and their messages in works that engage people at their emotions. It's magic to me and my desire to perform it myself is all-consuming. That's pretty much where this book of Ray-views comes from.

I love the "The Girl" books written by Stieg Larsson and continued by David Lagercrantz. Though they have their flaws, they express that love of figuring things out via research (especially via computer) and of publishing the results of that research for public consumption via the written word (books, magazines, websites). The books (especially Mr. Larsson's) show his characters' intensity as they go about this work. As they struggle to oppose corruption and criminality, they show the keyboard as being mightier than the sword. They honor intellectual work, but don't shy from its interface with physical action. In their own way, they honor geeks and further the nerd's revenge.

"The Girl" books are, among other things, a celebration of the modern artist with a keyboard. They take joy in the intellectual hero much as Elizabeth Kostova does in her novel, *The Historian* (see the "Beyond the Usual" category). Reading these books always makes me want to fire up my laptop computer and see what I can discover or create.

And then there are some novels that are technically good storytelling, but they simply fail to speak to me. This is the case with Whitley Strieber's *Alien Hunter*. It starts with a disappearance mystery, has a police detective protagonist, some colorful secondary characters, a sexy female sidekick, and aliens with technology thrown in. It was all enough to get it reproduced as a SyFy Channel series, but it struck me as too much of a formula. Now Mr. Strieber is best known for going public with his paranormal experiences that include "alien abduction," and I've followed

Ray-views

his career for some years. He infuses his fiction with what he's learned from his paranormal experiences and sometimes it works, and sometimes it doesn't. Stephen King says we can even learn from writing that doesn't grab us, and that's what I feel about *Alien Hunter*. It's at best a technical example in storytelling for me.

I find more pleasing examples of storytelling in a couple of collections of short stories by my old fiction writing teacher, John M. Floyd. Those books are *Deception* and *Fifty Mysteries* and they are pure and entertaining examples of writing in the mystery genre (though he does stretch some of them to Science Fiction and even Fantasy). Most have O'Henry type twist endings and *Fifty Mysteries* even leaves the solution out so that the reader can test his or her skills at deduction (the solutions are in a appendix). While I'm not a pure mystery fan, I think a good mystery thread can increase the interest of any story.

Historical fiction is a hot genre these days with a lot of good examples on the bestseller lists and being made into movies and series. One of my favorites is a 1999 novel by Steven Pressfield called, *Gates of Fire*. It's about the battle of Thermopylae in 480 AD where 300 Spartans, with a few thousand allies, held off the hordes of the invading Persian army. Mr. Pressfield does a good job of bringing the horrors of the battle and of the time period alive for the reader while providing some sympathetic characters to follow. As far as I know, this book was never made into a movie, but I think it should be.

Another one of those novels that doesn't grab me but that I find instructional is *The Haunted Mesa* by Louis L'Amour. It's interest to me is as a story written by a very genre-specific (Western) author that forays into a very different genre (science fiction). While I offer a number of technical criticisms of it in my Ray-view, I do admire Mr. L'Amour for making the attempt (just before he died).

And finally, I include an anthology of speculative fiction that I contributed to. So I'm biased in my Ray-view, but it does actually contain a lot of good stories (over 30). It's called, *While the Morning Stars Sing* and it was put together by Lyndon Perry, who ran a website of speculative fiction called, Residential Aliens (where Lyndon also published my short story, *Supernal*, which is part of my short story collection, *The Wider World*; so Lyndon has good taste). My contribution to the anthology is *Davis and the Goth* (which I revised for *The Wider World*). I read the stories in this collection from time-to-time for inspiration. They remind me of what I'm striving for.

There are a number of authors I admire, past and present, for the stories they tell and the lives they've led. I connect with them when I read

Storytelling

of their devotion to storytelling and to the written word. T. E. Lawrence ("Lawrence of Arabia") considered himself a writer and was very involved in the physical design of his book, *The Seven Pillars of Wisdom*. He even constructed a writing table for his cottage in England to suit his particular need to be relaxed while he wrote. Eric Blair (George Orwell) found he could only write well when his subject, fiction or not, was political. That certainly worked for him and I find I have similar feelings. I always feel sympathy for Mr. Blair when I remember that he was sick and dying as he worked on the manuscript for *1984*. His was a real deadline. Then there's James Hilton who wrote about a time (the 1930s) and themes of beauty and learning and travel with such passion that I would love to spend an evening with his characters from *Lost Horizon*.

And so many others. But I have to say I'm particularly fond of Homer, the classical "author" of *The Iliad* and *The Odyssey*. He was such a passionate storyteller that he didn't let blindness stop him. He wandered the streets of Athens just telling his stories to whomever would listen; and they're still told to this day. Now that's a storyteller.

The Girl Who Played With Fire

Author: Stieg Larsson
Publisher: Vintage
Publication date: 11/22/2011
Pages: 752
ISBN-13: 978-0307949509
Type: Fiction, Thriller, Suspense
Ray's rating: 4 stars
Characters: Lisbeth Salander, Mikael Blomkvist, Alexander Zalachenko, Jan Bublanski, Sonja Modig, Peter Teleborian, Erika Berger, Ronald Niedermann, Annika Giannini, Dragan Armansky, Gunnar Björck, Harriet Vanger, Holger Palmgren, Nils Bjurman, Miriam Wu

The first version of this review appeared on the www.goodreads.com and www.booklikes.com websites in August of 2014.

RAY-VIEW

THE GIRL WHO PLAYED WITH FIRE is the second novel in the late Stieg Larsson's *Millennium* series featuring the troubled, but brilliant, Lisbeth Salander. It is a thriller driven by a murder mystery as well as the mystery of "the evil" that set Salander's life course. There are psycho bad guys, corrupt health care professionals, a genetically modified killer, a task force of well and not-so-well intentioned cops, and a band of crusading journalists. All are tossed around in a ball of plot-threads that are wide-ranging before they are tied up (or at least brought into proximity). It's all held together by Mr. Larsson's depiction of Salander's quirky character, the mystery of her early life, and the threats on her current life, which will keep you reading to the end.

I have not read the first book in the series, *The Girl With the Dragon Tattoo*, but I did see the two movies made on it (the Swedish one and the American one with Daniel Craig). So I knew the story and the Salander character, but didn't appreciate what made the books popular until I read this one. In a nutshell, Mr. Larsson's formula is creating a mystery to be solved by a very eccentric but brilliant protagonist with the aid of a much more grounded and moral partner. It worked for Arthur Conan Doyle and it worked for Mr. Larsson.

Lisbeth Salander is probably as brilliant as Sherlock Holmes, though her deductive skills are augmented with computer hacking skills. She has

The Girl Who Played With Fire

a genius for mathematics that carries over into a genius for computer technology. She is an accomplished researcher but, like Sherlock Holmes, has minimal social skills. That social lack keeps her in trouble with coworkers and ultimately sabotages her budding relationship with her journalist partner, Mikael Blomkvist, in the first book. She sees life as black-and-white and is unforgiving. When she perceived Blomkvist as being unfaithful to her in the first book, she turned completely against him. For Salander, regaining trust is a slow, painful, process and it is an aching progression in *The Girl Who Played with Fire*. Even so, it is interesting to see how Salander and Blomkvist are still able to work together from a distance as they try to solve the story's mystery.

So working apart, and with different motivations, Salander and Blomkvist apply their skills to solving the murder of two of Blomkvist's journalist friends and of Salander's sleazy guardian--murders for which Salander becomes the prime suspect. This murder mystery thread is kicked off by Salander's guardian, Nils Bjurman, scheming to get free from Salander's blackmailing of him. She did this to be free of his brutal exploitation of her that occurred in the first book.

That thread, however, is preceded by a chapter describing Salander's time in the Caribbean solving a mini-murder mystery, having a physical relationship with a teenaged boy, and weathering a hurricane. Nothing of that situation or its characters is raised again in the rest of the book, so it may have been to show a softer side of Salander before the main plot, or it just planted seeds for something else. Anyway, it struck me as bit of misdirection.

Once the main plot is kicked off, however, it becomes another engrossing read, for the most part. It is carried along by Salander's computer hacks (which struck me as pretty accurately depicted for pre-2004 technology), Blomkvist's journalistic research (and it's interesting to see the editorial workings of *Millennium* magazine; at least it was to me), and the investigations of the police task force. In all this, there are a lot of characters to keep up with, especially among the police. The major ones coalesce into characters with plot threads, but many remain just names. In fact, there were so many characters with small threads entwining the main cable, that I nearly lost the flow a few times. The omniscient point-of-view added to the sprawling effect, with the POV changing sometimes from sentence-to-sentence. It never got too bad, however, and it was worth hanging with.

Part of the story involves sex-trade trafficking and the reader learns a bit about that. We see that it's mostly done by low-level gangs of low-brow criminals rather than a high-powered mafia. Prostitutes are created from impoverished young women taken, or enticed, from eastern European countries to the more advanced ones, like Sweden. That creation is done brutally and provides a key plot element. But then there are sections where Mr. Larsson describes some very open-minded sexual attitudes among his characters, including Salander. They're so open-minded they seem unreal, but it may have simply been a device to contrast attitudes between regular people and the criminals. Still, some of Mr. Larsson's characters engage in some very casual sex to the point that it didn't seem believable, and seems out-of-character even for Salander. Of course, maybe that's just the way it is in Sweden.

My other little criticism is that there are long sections where the plot is advanced only by a lot of dialogue among characters with little action. I think Mr. Larsson took this a tad too far, but not enough for me to abandon the book. The dialogue is a lot of telling-not-showing, technically speaking. On the other hand, Mr. Larsson was skilled enough to get away with it, as the conversations were generally interesting. It's like listening in on professionals discussing an engrossing topic.

The book's story is told in four parts. Each part begins with a mathematical rule or theorem, implied as coming from a book of mathematics that Salander is reading. I supposed Mr. Larsson was making a connection from the math to the section of his story it headed. If that's the case, I'm not mathematical enough to appreciate it.

The last third of the book turns very action-oriented and leads to a thrilling and satisfying conclusion that is enhanced by Mr. Larsson making Salander a Christ-figure. It took some guts for him to make that come off well, but he did it.

The Girl Who Played with Fire is a continuation of *The Girl with the Dragon Tattoo* more so than a sequel. The characters evolve, especially Lisbeth Salander, who does so in a believable and engaging way. She is already a new classic in literary characters and is the great strength of Mr. Larsson's *Millennium* series. I expect she'll be around, and imitated, for a while.

The Girl Who Kicked the Hornet's Nest

Author: Stieg Larsson
Publisher: Vintage
Publication date: 02/21/2012
Pages: 832
ISBN-13: 978-0307742537
Type: Fiction, Thriller, Suspense
Ray's rating: 4 stars
Characters: Lisbeth Salander, Mikael Blomkvist, Alexander Zalachenko, Jan Bublanski, Sonja Modig, Peter Teleborian, Erika Berger, Ronald Niedermann, Annika Giannini, Dragan Armansky, Monica Figuerola, Torsten Edklinth, Dr. Anders Jonasson, Gunnar Björck

The first version of this review appeared on the www.goodreads.com and www.booklikes.com websites in September of 2015.

RAY-VIEW

THE GIRL WHO KICKED THE HORNET'S NEST is the third book in Stieg Larsson's Millennium series of novels concerning his literary cult creation, Lisbeth Salander. The series has generated at least two films and a rabid following. It's a deserved following, in my opinion, because Mr. Larsson came up with an updated version of Holmes-and-Watson and made it work. Unfortunately, Mr. Larsson's success was posthumous.

The Millennium trilogy is a single, three-part, work, although the last two parts are more connected than the first. I won't do spoilers or get to much into the twisting plot, but the book teasers do tell you that this story begins with Salander in the hospital with a bullet in her head. That should catch a potential reader's interest as well as it serves to carry readers from the second to the third book. I thought it was gutsy of Mr. Larsson to kill off, then resurrect, his popular protagonist in the second book. Of course, that further cements the series' connection to Sherlock Holmes, who was also killed-off and brought back by A. C. Doyle (though not in the same book). But Salander has problems besides her head injury. She is suspected of a triple homicide, sought by a villainous motorcycle gang, threatened with being locked up in a psych unit by rogue government authorities, has put the closest things she has to friends in danger, and is

Ray-views

cut-off from all computer access. That's good stage-setting for a lot of drama.

And that drama largely concerns just who Lisbeth Salander is: where she came from and why she is the way she is. Mr. Larsson does answer these questions and they are nature-nurture answers with the answers coming down mostly on the nurture side. Salander's upbringing was, to say the least, dysfunctional. That is hinted at in the first book along with the institutionalized abuse she suffered, but the reasons behind it all are revealed in this last book.

That reasoning concerns some intricate plotting at the core of which is an "unofficial" section of the Swedish security agency, SAPO (which seems to be an FBI-CIA look-alike), and its dealings to protect a Russian defector during the cold war. The agency's machinations (or at least of its rogue part) to protect the defector lead directly to the abuses suffered by Salander. Of course, they also lead to her creation as an antihero crime-fighter (with a particular bent to work against woman abusers). With that foundation, Mr. Larsson unwinds his story, and it is a long unwinding.

The strength of *The Girl Who Kicked the Hornet's Nest*, as with the other books in the series, is undoubtedly it's protagonist, Lisbeth Salander. Though she spends a lot of the novel in the hospital, she does finally come to her trademark computer skills and antisocial behavior. She even almost accepts friendships, though she fights the impulse. And though barely topping five feet in height, she still kicks butt when she needs to.

Another strength is the involved plot (though there is also a down side to that). It is entwined from many threads that connect a defecting Russian psychopath, a secret Swedish agency, and official corruption to Salander's dysfunctional childhood. Mr. Larsson comes at this plot from a number of different angles and in the process shows us a lot about the functionings of the Swedish government, the Swedish police, mental institutions, and the workings of large publications (at least Swedish ones). The latter was the most interesting for me. That, along with the sections when Salander is working her computer magic, provide inspiration to me for when I'm writing and makes me feel like I'm doing something. Maybe that's also a lot of Salander's appeal. Very few authors have been able to make sympathetic characters out of computer hackers and it's generally done with an antihero protagonist. Mr. Larsson does that with Salander, but goes further to create a truly interesting character.

Mikael Blomkvist is the foil to Salander. His crusading, womanizing, straightness stands in contrast to Salander's bend-all-the-rules approach to everything. It is her brilliance coming from her dysfunction, however, that earns her respect from those who care enough to see it. It also earns

The Girl Who Kicked the Hornet's Nest

her their loyalty and abiding friendship, even though she is not comfortable in accepting them. Blomkvist is the foremost of these loyal friends and he provides the establishment support she needs to get by without becoming an outlaw. And the fact that Mr. Larsson made him a journalist--a writer--makes him the Watson character who can provide the documentary evidence of Salander's exploits for posterity.

I have, however, some criticisms of *The Girl Who Kicked the Hornet's Nest*. Mostly, the book is too long. A long book is OK if it's long with storytelling. Unfortunately, *Hornet's Nest* is long with repetitions of plot threads (the same story section told from two or more viewpoints; in some stories this is OK, but it's overdone here) and needless banter. Regarding the latter, there's a part where Berger is being given an overview of the security system she's had installed in her house and the talk goes on for several pages. For what was necessary for the plot, it could have been dispensed with in a paragraph. There are numerous examples of this, where characters go on talking about peripheral items like relationships and politics which have scant connection to the plot or anybody's character. It makes the narrative grind down to a point of prompting the reader to give up.

Also, Salander is in the hospital for about the first half of the book and she's not doing enough during that time. Even worse, there are long stretches where Salander is nowhere in sight. The other characters, except maybe Blomkvist, cannot support the story like she can. Indeed, like with Sherlock Holmes, the story is very secondary to the character of its quirky protagonist. This book should have been greatly condensed around the characters of Salander and Blomkvist. Now all those sections where we see the workings of the police task force, and the SAPO section, and the magazine and newspapers were neat in their place, but they were too long and overshadowed Salander and Blomkvist when they should not have.

The "Note About the Author" at the end of the book says Mr. Larsson delivered the manuscripts (presumably to the publisher) for the entire trilogy shortly before his death. This makes me wonder if he actually completed them (although I suspect he had the very last sentence written long before the second two books were done). An awful lot of the "excess" I've noted for the second two books sounds like backstory to me, and a lack of editing. If that's true, then Mr. Larsson joined the likes of George Orwell in hurrying to complete a manuscript before his death. There's certainly nothing wrong with that, but I think a sympathetic editor would have done better justice to the manuscripts.

Or maybe the Swedish have longer attention spans and they like their novels that way. Regardless, I think the genius in Mr. Larsson's work is

Ray-views

his main character. Watching Lisbeth Salander work and strike out against her exploiters is the fun of the books. It is great fun watching Ms Salander solve a mystery using her computer (like watching Mr. Holmes do it with his computer-like intellect) and being supported by her faithful, journalistic, companion (same as Holmes). In his Millennium series of novels, Stieg Larsson has created a literary character who is destined to become a classic. It is a shame that he is no longer around to continue Ms Salander's exploits, but then, maybe that torch will be handed off.

The Girl in the Spider's Web

Author: David Lagercrantz
Publisher: Knopf
Publication date: 09/01/2015
Pages: 432
ISBN-13: 978-0-385-35428-8
Type: Fiction, Suspense, International Mystery & Crime
Ray's rating: 4 stars
Characters: Lisbeth Salander, Mikael Blomkvist, Frans Balder, August Balder, Gabriella Grane, Jan Bublanski, Sonja Modig, Erika Berger, Ed Needham

The first version of this review appeared on the www.goodreads.com and www.booklikes.com websites in October of 2015.

RAY-VIEW

IN THIS fourth installment of the *Millennium* series of novels begun by Stieg Larsson, Lisbeth Salander (antihero computer/math genius) and her sidekick Mikael Blomkvist (idealistic investigative journalist) take on a coalition of the Russian Mafia, rogue elements of the NSA, criminal anti-hackers, and an "evil twin," in their quest to reveal government crimes, solve the murder of a prominent computer scientist, exact revenge, and fight off a hostile takeover of *Millennium* magazine. As with the first three novels, there's a lot going on for our heroes to handle.

But I think the big question that greeted the release of this book was whether the author, David Lagercrantz, was able to continue the series created by the late Stieg Larsson and maintain the integrity of the storyline and characters that Mr. Larsson made so popular. The consensus seems to be that he did, and I have to agree. I noted one reviewer who said she felt like she was reading Mr. Larsson's writing and I have say that I felt that too. Overall, I would say that Mr. Lagercrantz must have loved the first three books and did a thorough job in his research of them. His initial foray into the world of Lisbeth Salander is pretty much seamless.

Now in my opinion, *The Girl in the Spider's Web* is technically better written than Mr. Larsson's books. Both the plotting and the prose are tighter and that resulted in a book that is 250 to 400 pages shorter than Mr. Larsson's books. I think the tighter prose is not because Mr. Lagercrantz is a better writer, but more likely because Mr. Larsson was pushed by ill health to get his manuscripts submitted, and they weren't adequately edited. That is strictly my opinion, but I base it on that so much of Mr. Larsson's prose was sheer exposition and large sections were even irrelevant to the storyline, reading like backstory. Mr. Lagercrantz's version, by and large, eliminates those issues.

In spite of the technical difficulties of the first three books, they established a setting and characters that garnered a global host of ardent fans who elevated the antihero protagonist to cult status. That made producing a fourth book a gutsy proposition, but one that I believe Mr. Lagercrantz pulled off.

In *Spider's Web* Lisbeth Salander is satisfyingly edgy, brilliant, and antisocial. She has reconciled with Blomkvist enough to work with him, though still from a distance. We learn more about her history and it is a believable extension of what was revealed in the previous three books (I would assume it all came from Mr. Larsson's notes). We also see her relate to a child who is a mathematical savant. The boy, August Balder, is in some ways a reflection of Salander as a child and she recognizes that. The scenes with them are an interesting counterpoint to Salander's more hard-bitten ones where she is flouting authority or being vengeful.

Salander's foil, Mikael Blomkvist, is also presented true-to-the-first-books. He is still idealistic in pursuing journalism that "makes a difference," though he finds it tough resting on past laurels in a time when print magazines are going all electronic. Faced with becoming irrelevant, he must also endure the threat of his beloved Millennium magazine being cheapened, out of the need to obtain a financial rescue from a big publishing company led by an old rival.

Blomkvist has obtained a level of fame from the exposes of rich people and his writing about high-profile crimes as told in the previous books. He is uncomfortable with his fame, however, and concerned with losing it only to the extent it might hurt Millennium. He is ever loyal to Salander and he gets involved in the mystery of the computer scientist's murder only when he learns of a connection between the man and Salander.

Most of the other characters established in the first books are here as well, and all struck me as true to their creation. Mr. Lagercrantz doesn't dwell on them as much, but that struck me as good because there is no need to. Still we still see the workings of the local police as well as of SAPO (Swedish Intelligence Agency) as they deal with the story's murders and mysteries. Here, Mr. Lagercrantz added an interesting aspect with the existential crisis undergone by the police inspector, Jan Bublanski. It adds a certain philosophical note to everything and might say something along

The Girl in the Spider's Web

the lines of "what's the point of all this?" A similar note is sounded with a new character, Gabriella Grane, of SAPO, through whom we get a word on the book's theme:

She shuddered at the creeping realization that we live in a twisted world where everything, both big and small, is subject to surveillance, and where anything worth money will always be exploited.

That might also be the theme of the whole series.

Of course, these books deal a lot with computer technology, given the vocation of the protagonist. Mr. Larsson's books were very true to that technology at the level it existed at around 2004. Mr. Lagercrantz's book brings it up to the current time (2015). While he does a good job of that, where I think he doesn't do as well as Mr. Larsson is in showing us Salander working at it. That is, we see her at her laptop, hacking and researching, but we're watching her from a greater distance than we were when Mr. Larsson was describing such scenes. Somehow, I got a greater feeling for Salander's passion for her work and felt the dynamic of her pounding that keyboard for answers in a way more visceral than shown in *Spider's Web*. I could say the same for the workings of the publishing world in those scenes with Blomkvist at Millennium. It is there, but I felt it more in Mr. Larsson's prose. This is a minor criticism, however, and I expect most fans won't notice it.

Regarding the updating of the series' storyline, I have to give Mr. Lagercrantz kudos for attacking the issue of unaccountable surveillance by government agencies. He even places scenes inside the NSA and, via one notable character, pits the NSA against Salander. But in doing so, he follows Mr. Larsson's lead in letting the NSA and other government agencies off too lightly. Their faults are seen as coming from "rogue elements" or "bad apples" rather than being systemic. Maybe the Swedes have more faith in authority than I do.

It also seems to me that, in spite of the tighter prose, there is a lot of exposition in the narrative--telling not showing. Again, it's not as bad as in the first books but it is noticeable. Maybe it's a Swedish thing or a result of translation, but I thought it was too much and it cost a star in my rating.

At the ending of *Spider's Web*, there is a sense of "wrapping up" that is satisfying, but I don't think it signals the end of the series. Actually, about midway through the book I was beginning to wonder of the story threads spun by Mr. Larsson were going to wind up with this book. Then Camilla Salander popped up and was developed just enough to add the promise for a worthy antagonist for Lisbeth. That could carry another book or two if handled well.

It has got to be intimidating to pick up writing on a fiction series that has developed a worldwide cult following, but it seems David Lagercrantz was the man for the job. I expect most fans will be pleased with his results.

Alien Hunter

Author: Whitley Strieber
Publisher: Tor Books
Publication date: 08/13/2013
Pages: 320
ISBN-13: 978-0765331533
Type: Fiction, Science Fiction
Ray's rating: 3 stars
Characters: Erroll (Flynn) Carroll, Diana Glass, MacAdoo (Mac) Terrell

The first version of this review appeared on the www.goodreads.com and www.booklikes.com websites in April of 2014.

RAY-VIEW

POLICE detective Flynn Carroll wakes in the middle of the night to find that his pregnant wife has disappeared without a trace. He reports her as missing to his department and his cop friends search, but the case looks like she is a runaway and it eventually goes cold. But Flynn keeps pursuing her case along with many other similar ones until he becomes such an expert in missing persons that he attracts the attention of a secret US federal agency. He is recruited by this agency, which has extraterrestrial connections, and hunts down his wife's abductor who is, of course, an alien.

This is the premise of Whitley Strieber's *Alien Hunter* novel. It's basically a cop thriller with an extraterrestrial angle thrown in. That alien aspect of the story is the most interesting part of it for me, simply because it reflects Whitley's experiences with apparent alien contact that he has documented in his nonfiction books. So his depiction of the aliens and how they operate has the feel of UFO anecdotes--mysterious lights, frightening entities glimpsed in the dark, and time-condensed abductions. This adds a "reality" to the alien scenes that make them interesting beyond the usual such in science fiction stories, but they become more "typical" when he gets down to his characters' actual interaction with the aliens. That is, the aliens become less alien and more human in their criminality.

The storyline, despite the alien angle, is pretty much typical for the cop thriller genre--a hard-boiled detective goes searching for the abductor of his wife, finds a sexy partner along the way, handles guns, flies planes, talks tough, and fights it out with the bad guy in the end. Now if you're

Ray-views

just really into this genre, and a lot of people are, then you may very well like this book, especially if you're open to the science fiction angle. But it failed for me just because I didn't find the lead character interesting. I didn't find any of the characters interesting, actually, though Mr. Strieber did throw a slight twist at the end concerning the sexy partner that kind of broke the mold.

My best takeaways from this book were the parts of the alien scenes that I detected as being from real UFO stories and from Mr. Strieber's experiences. Also the aliens' use of genetically engineered animals was an interesting component that could have been enlarged. And more, in the midst of the usual thriller plot, Mr. Strieber adds an observation that should have been a major theme, but that lost much from not being supported with interesting action and sympathetic characters. That was the feeling of isolation in people who have a knowledge of bizarre and appalling situations that are not suspected by the people around them. This is expressed in *Alien Hunter* in Flynn Carroll's thoughts as he considered the people milling around him in a store:

He understood the origin of Diana's inner distance. It was having secret knowledge of a larger world that did it. They were innocent, he was not.

I considered this the story's highpoint, and the rest of it didn't measure up.

I suspect that a lot of *Alien Hunter*'s shortcomings are from the fact that it will be dramatized as a series on the *SyFy Channel*. It feels like it was written for that (or heavily edited by *SyFy*) and so it couldn't rise above a certain level. As such, it only made it to three stars for me.

Deception

Author: John M. Floyd
Publisher: Dogwood Press
Publication date: April 2013
Pages: 328
ISBN-13: 9780983538646
Type: Fiction, Short Stories, Mystery
Ray's rating: 5 stars

The first version of this review appeared on the www.goodreads.com website in July of 2013.

RAY-VIEW

MYSTERY lovers will love this book. Especially mystery lovers that live in the southern US as Mr. Floyd lends the ambiance of that locale to the stories in this collection--sometimes overtly and sometimes subtly. His fanbase appreciates the pure mystery genre of "puzzle" in his stories with surprise endings. These are basted with police procedurals and seasoned with local color and characters to create a pleasing literary stew.

Deception is a compilation of 30 short stories that are all solidly in the mystery genre, although they do range in settings from contemporary ("Weekend Getaway") to westerns ("The Noon Stage," "Redemption") to science fiction ("Travelers") and even a touch of fantasy ("Mythic Heights").

The stories vary a lot in length and so Mr. Floyd shows his ability to tell a story within word counts. "Frankie" is a flash fiction told in 3 pages with no dialogue, but has a tight plot about an unlikely hero. "Redemption" is the longest at 52 pages with a more involved plot. It is a western with a light romance (reminds me of *Gunsmoke*) and a "cowboy" protagonist who attacks a murder mystery like *Hec Ramsey* (an old TV series of the western mystery genre). Speaking of TV mystery programs, Mr. Floyd has a character, Angela Potts, who is a retired schoolteacher and amateur sleuth who appears in many of his stories. I believe he could do a novel or two with her and the associated characters and settings.

There is a high moral tone to all of these stories with an emphasis is on crime-solving rather than the crime. Mr. Floyd is more concerned with following a sympathetic character through the process of figuring out "what happened" (or "what to do") rather than dwelling on the depravity of a killer. "Turnabout" is a strong example of this where even a criminal protagonist has redeeming qualities.

And there is a strong "twist" element that ends most of the stories. Sometimes it's a sheer play on words and assumptions that catch you by surprise in the final sentences, such as in "The Noon Stage" and "Just Passing Through." Mr. Floyd has built his reputation on doing this and it works.

My second favorite story in this collection is "Travelers" because it is a soft science fiction with a puzzle plot that is worthy of a *Twilight Zone* or *Night Gallery* episode.

My favorite story was "Deception," the last one in the book and the second longest. It's not as hardcore mystery as the other stories, but it does pull you along and keep you guessing to a satisfying ending, and the setting ambiance is very familiar to me.

Some time ago, in a review for a short story anthology, I wrote: "The best short stories are those that touch us in our personal spaces--like a song that vibrates our heart chords with just the right melody, meter, and words." I believe Mr. Floyd has accomplished that with this collection of stories. If you love clever whodunit (or "howdunit") stories with tight plots twisting and turning to unexpected endings, you'll love the stories in *Deception*.

Fifty Mysteries: The Angela Files

Author: John M Floyd
Publisher: Dogwood Press
Publication date: 10/29/2014
Pages: 224
ISBN-13: 0983538670
Type: Fiction, Short Stories, Mystery
Ray's rating: 5 stars
Characters: Angela Potts, Charles "Chunky" Jones, Fred Prewitt, Sally

The first version of this review appeared on the www.goodreads.com and www.booklikes.com websites in November of 2014.

RAY-VIEW

FIFTY MYSTERIES: THE ANGELA FILES is John M. Floyd's brain-teasing collection of short mystery stories built around the characters of Sheriff Charles "Chunky" Jones and amateur sleuth, Angela Potts. They live in a small, unnamed, southern (US) town where they cooperate in solving mysteries of the criminal sort.

Angela Potts is a retired grade school teacher with a passion for puzzle-solving that has made her an unofficial consultant for the local police. Whether the crime be a murder or a puppy theft, she spots the tiny detail or makes the obscure connection that solves the mystery.

Sheriff Jones is Angela's former underachieving student who has come to respect, and even rely upon, Ms Potts' detective abilities. Though he can be cantankerous at times, and even dismissive of Potts, he always comes around to letting her do her thing to get the crime-solving done.

The crimes this duo tackles are presented in *Fifty Mysteries* as prose puzzles of the sort that are at the heart of storytelling in the crime mystery genre. Wasting no words (the stories average 4.4 pages with little variation) Mr. Floyd lays out the crime facts, plants clues and red herrings, and shows Jones and Potts working to a resolution (usually accomplished by Ms Potts, hence the subtitle: *The Angela Files*). A key element of that resolution, however, is left out and the reader is invited to supply it from clues offered in the story.

That element might be the perpetrator's identity or how Ms Potts or Sheriff Jones deducted it. To guide their deductions, at the end of each story readers are prompted with questions such as:

Ray-views

Why did Angela already suspect that George Glenn was the killer?

What gave Martin Russell away?

Which of the three young men was lying?

The answers are in the back of the book. This "interactive" format makes *Fifty Mysteries* very much a puzzle book and so is not a passive read if you try to solve the mysteries, as devotees of the genre will surely do. I found myself reading very deliberately, trying to evaluate the clues and spot the key inconsistencies as I went. It usually took a thoughtful rereading for me to find the solution, which I did about half the time.

Fifty Mysteries will exercise your detective muscle, which is the fun of mystery stories. The method for doing so, advocated by Angela Potts in agreement with Sherlock Holmes, is to observe rather than just look. And what Angela is looking and listening for is inconsistencies. As she says to Sheriff Jones (who is still learning from her):

"...I just watch for inconsistencies...All liars aren't lawbreakers, but most lawbreakers are liars. You have to listen for things that don't add up."

The 50 mysteries are set in a specific universe that we come to know as we follow the stories and the characters that live there. That universe (southern small town USA) is a vital part of the storytelling (think Sherlock Holmes and late 19th century London) and Mr. Floyd is very true to it. We come to enjoy the repartee between Sheriff Jones and Ms Potts, and appreciate their history and ongoing student-teacher relationship. Now these stories are economical in the telling so there isn't a lot of explicit character development since the emphasis is on "the puzzle," still, we can infer a few things.

It seems that Ms Potts has ingratiated herself with the sheriff to the point that he has overcome his initial resistance to her "meddling" and now considers her a part of his staff (he even says as much at one point). He brings her to crime scenes to get her opinion, lets her handle dispatch, and makes arrests based on her deductions. She is even referred to a couple of times as an "Investigative consultant." At other times, though, Ms Potts' successes wear on Jones' ego to the point that he doubts himself. He feels he is playing second fiddle to his fifth grade teacher. This really only surfaces in one story (#36) but it's the sheriff's most touching moment for me:

Fifty Mysteries: The Angela Files

"...When something interesting happens, something serious, you always solve the case."

In mystery #44, Mr. Floyd tells the story from the viewpoint of the perpetrator. This is the only one where he does this and it's an engaging contrast to the other stories. Seeing the perp's chagrin at his own inconsistencies and his bewilderment at Ms Potts' presence provides an interesting perspective on the Potts and Jones characters and their relationship established in the other stories:

The police arrived within minutes. To his surprise, a gray-haired lady showed up with Sheriff Jones and his deputy.

Mr. Floyd has longer treatments of Angela Potts and "Chunky" Jones in his other works and these characters' popularity among readers is what led to them being the exclusive sleuths in this book. So sit back and enjoy their mutual annoyance and admiration as they work together to deduce the truth from the twisting machinations of criminal minds. And try your hand at solving these 50 mysteries in the storied, sunbaked South, where crimes abound, everyone eats at Roscoe's, and the sheriff can still learn from a retired school teacher who has found her second career in listening for people to "say something wrong."

Gates of Fire

Author: Steven Pressfield
Publisher: Random House Publishing Group
Publication date: 9/28/1999
Pages: 480
ISBN-13: 9780553580532
Type: Fiction, Historical Fiction, War
Ray's rating: 4 stars
Characters: Leonidas, Xerxes I of Persia, Xeones, Dienekes, Polynikes

The first version of this review appeared on the www.goodreads.com website in September of 2012.

RAY-VIEW

    I GENERALLY don't care for stories that glorify war, but then, war is a large part of the human condition and so is a legitimate subject for examination. In *Gates of Fire* Steven Pressfield offers an engrossing account of the classical era battle of Thermopylae.
    The facts of the battle are dramatic enough--300 Spartan warriors with a few thousand allied troops withstood for seven days the onslaught of the invading Persian army numbering in the hundreds of thousands (or two million by ancient accounts that, while dramatic, aren't considered reliable). Pressfield fleshes out these basic facts along with the account of battle by Herodutus, into a compelling tale of heroism in the face of insuperable odds.
    Pressfield's story is told by Xeones, a surviving member of the Greek defenders. He is the young squire of the Spartan knight, Dienekes, and is taken from the battlefield by the victorious Persians to recount his tale of the defenders for their king Xerxes. In doing so, he tells his own tale of woe and destitution that brought him into Spartan service. His story brings in that of the other principals of the battle, including Dienekes, Polynikes, and King Leonidas, as Xeo's life touched theirs. In this telling, the reader gets a wide-angle view of life in classical times, with all it's desperation, cruelty, and rural simplicity. It's a view through the eyes of a host of sympathetic characters that draws in the reader so that we care about these people's fates, even through the inevitable loss at the climatic battle.

Gates of Fire

This interweaved story of individuals, with all the loves and hatreds between them, is what makes Pressfield's novel so much more than a mere military history or the recounting of a battle. Some reviewers have been critical of the "lofty" language Pressfield uses in his dialogue, but I don't believe that's a warranted criticism. Reproducing classical speech requires that or it just doesn't work. Maybe Shakespeare just set the bar that high, but the dialogue in this book is still less Shakespearean than the Starz *Spartacus* series (and it works very well in that series). I think it enhances the satisfying depth of storytelling with historical fact that makes *Gates of Fire* the definitive retelling of the battle of Thermopylae, as opposed to the idiotic, video game ripoff movie, *300*.

As I said, I don't care for stories that glorify war, but I don't think *Gates of Fire* glorifies war so much as it does the Greek warriors that fought at Thermopylae. Pressfield doesn't shrink from showing the horrors of war--the lawless brutality and the appalling mechanics of fighting that requires the enemy to be hacked to death. In that regard, the story echoes Shakespeare's *Henry V* in depicting war as a multi-faceted thing (Shakespeare does it better, but that's no indictment of Mr. Pressfield).

Gates of Fire works as a historical novel and I highly recommend it for its sense of history and sympathetic characters. And I think it would make a great movie.

The Haunted Mesa

Author: Louis L'Amour
Publisher: Random House Publishing Group
Publication date: 4/28/1988
Pages: 448
ISBN-13: 9780553270228
Type: Fiction, Science Fiction, Western
Ray's rating: 3 stars
Characters: Mike Ragland, Erik Hokart

The first version of this review appeared on the www.goodreads.com website in September of 2013.

RAY-VIEW

MIKE RAGLAND is the hero and sole point-of-view of Louis L'Amour's "science fiction" novel, *The Haunted Mesa*. When Mike receives a letter from a friend, Erik Hokart, asking him to meet him in the New Mexico desert where he's building a house on a mesa, Mike answers the call, spurred by the letter's sense of urgency. He makes the rendezvous but Erik does not. Erik is missing, but he has left Mike a record of events that led up to his disappearance in the form of a "daybook" journal delivered to him by a mysterious woman who seems not of this world. Mike is an investigator of things paranormal, best known for exposing charlatans. He's an author, world traveler, ex-cowboy, and general roustabout--just the sort of knowledgeable tough guy to tackle the mystery of Erik's disappearance with its other-worldly undertones, and fight off any evil-doers involved.

In the course of Mike's investigation, he is aided by the local sheriff and followed by thugs who seem unfamiliar with the way our world works. Using Erik's journal as a guide, Mike follows a trail that leads to portals between dimensions, a ruined citadel containing a maze, "enforcers" that are unused to being resisted, a chief bad guy with steely fingers, a lost Indian tribe, giant lizards, and even a sasquatch makes an appearance. All of the action, even in the other dimension, is set in the US desert southwest where Mike figures out the riddles, the maze, and shoots-and-punches bad guys and lizards to find his friend and win his Indian princess.

The Haunted Mesa

The Haunted Mesa is generally listed as science fiction in the bibliography of Mr. L'Amour's works, though I would consider it more fantasy-western or speculative. It was apparently his last novel (published a scant two months before his death in 1988) and I suspect it was a break from most of what he had written before. He was, along with Zane Grey, a preeminent writer of the American western genre. Many of his works were made into movies and TV (e.g., John Wayne's *Hondo*) and he still has a passionate following.

Though set in contemporary times, I found *The Haunted Mesa* to be a thorough western in ambiance, theme, and structure despite it's speculative elements. And I mean "western" in the classic sense, like in John Ford movies and early 1960's television. The conflicts are very black-and-white, good-and-bad, with NO shades of gray. The point-of-view is with the protagonist, Mike Ragland, all the way through. Other characters come and go, but the tale told is Ragland's, with no input from anybody else. He makes his way through the adventure two-fisted and armed--"He had no desire to kill anything," but then again, "nor did he have any desire to be a chance victim." So the bad guys (other dimensional Indians in this story) fall like regular Indians in a John Wayne film. We don't know why they're bad, they just are, and they're led by a guy who is the worst, also for no apparent reason.

If I'm sounding down on the book, it's mostly because I'm really not a fan of this genre. I read the book just because I wanted to see what a Louis L'Amour book was like and it was pretty much what I expected. So while this kind of western is not my favorite brand of storytelling, I realize that it *is* for a lot of people. The aspects of the story I described in the last paragraph are why many people *like* L'Amour's works. I understand that and, if you're one of those people, you'll probably like *The Haunted Mesa*. And I would recommend it to you because I suspect Mr. L'Amour stepped out of his comfort zone with this work and offered his fans some food for thought.

The main morsel of that thought food is the idea that the "paranormal" is really just the "normal" beyond the limits of what we've figured out. "There are more things in heaven and earth," in other words. On this point, Mr. L'Amour and I are in complete agreement, and he says it well:

> *The terms we use for what is considered supernatural are woefully inadequate. Beyond such terms as ghost, specter, poltergeist, angel, devil, or spirit, might there not be something more our purposeful blindness has prevented us from understanding?*

Ray-views

Still, there are, in my opinion, technical problems with the story that kept me from giving it more than three stars.

First, as I said, the POV never leaves the protagonist. That's not bad in itself, it's just that it underscores the one-dimensionality of this storytelling. The story really needs the viewpoints of some other characters to give it some depth and to better engage the reader.

Second, the conflicts were too black-and-white. This builds on my first point in that the secondary characters, especially the "bad" characters, have no depth and in some cases, barely react. The "other world" and its inhabitants are just bad for no reason (other than some intimation that their civilization had simply degenerated).

Third, there is not enough feel for "place." The story is set in the desert southwest, which with its red-rock canyons and stately mesas is a dramatic place for someone not accustomed to it. It's barely described in the story. We're told that the view from the top of the mesa is beautiful, but the words don't show it to us or let us feel the characters interaction with their environment. For this setting that is a big omission, especially with a story that's not meant to be geared exclusively for fans of westerns.

Fourth, the romance was totally not believable. I guess that's part of the genre. The women are there as rewards for the cowboy hero defeating the bad guys, but Ragland seems to fall in love out of nowhere--when the object of his "affection" is not even around. When she is around, she doesn't react much to him in that way, and when he starts calling her "honey" it just sounds condescending. Oh well, I guess that's why cowboys kissed their horses at the end of the old movies.

Fifth, Indians are depicted as savage and/or backwards. I won't belabor this point, I could write scads about it. Western fans would say that the cowboy hero has a lot of respect for the Indians. I would argue, however, that the classic cowboy hero's respect for the Indian is really just a "white man's burden" kind of condescension.

Sixth, there were too many passages where Ragland's interior questionings were explicitly stated. There was far too much of this:

What was he doing here, anyway? Why was he not back at Tamarron, going down to the San Juan Room for breakfast in a normal, sensible, attractive world? What was he doing out here at the end of everything?

Some is OK, but too much is telling the reader what to think and how he should be reacting to the story. It amounts to "telling" and not "showing."

The Haunted Mesa

Those are my criticisms but let me add that Mr. L'Amour was a good writer. He made a living at it for most of his life, writing a genre at a time when there was a big market for it and establishing a large and loyal following. This is apparent in his prose, which he handles capably and is able to turn a compelling phrase here and there:

There were ancient mysteries, old gods who retired into the canyons to await new believers who would bring them to life once more.

Phrases like that are what kept me reading to the end.

The Haunted Mesa didn't do it for me, but if you're a fan of the classic western and are open to a little expansion on the basic storylines into speculative realms, you'll like this book.

While the Morning Stars Sing

Author: Edited by Lyndon Perry
Publisher: ResAlien Press
Publication date: 07/01/2011
Pages: 256
ISBN-13: 9781463722326
Type: Speculative Fiction, Short Stories, Anthology
Ray's rating: 5 stars

The first version of this review appeared on the www.goodreads.com website in August of 2015.

RAY-VIEW

    THE BEST short stories are those that touch us in our personal spaces--like a song that vibrates our heart chords with just the right melody, meter, and words. They speak to us at that place where we're the most receptive for a given place and time.
    The collection of stories, poems, and illustrations bound within the covers of *While the Morning Stars Sing* will speak to you in that way if you're open to speculative musings about life with spiritual themes. They are generally very overt in following their genres: whether science fiction (*We Are Us* by T.J. McIntyre), horror (*The Blood of Thousands* by Steve Goble), fantasy (*Patron Saint* by Breanna Teintze), romance (*Butterflies Dancing* by Rachel Thomson), or even folklore (*A Fisherman's Tale* by Pete Mesling).
    Each has harmonizing chords, some louder than others, that enhance the melody of their narrative with a tone evoking deeper meanings, like a vocal backed by organ or choir.
    I especially liked *Fragments* by Aaron Polson for it's buildup of mystery that ends with an aching heart-tug, and *Mound of Mud* by Fred Warren for its simple humor and appealing characters operating within a fantastic situation; and *One Blink For Yes* by Margaret Karmazin because it proves that someone besides me has read *Journeys Out of the Body*.
    The "spiritually infused" theme of the collection is an excellent orchestration by the editor, Lyndon Perry, and aptly resonates with the stories published on his website, Residential Aliens.
    My own contribution to the anthology is *Davis and the Goth*, which is my (embellished) reminiscence about being bullied in Bible Camp with the fervent desire for deliverance. It ends with a twist in the very last

While the Morning Stars Sing

sentence that you probably would had to have grown up in a fundamentalist church to really appreciate.

I love that my story is part of this collection and am honored to be allowed in among such outstanding storytellers.

So, in a nutshell, I highly recommend this anthology of speculative fiction. Buy it as you would buy an album of pleasing music. Read each story and poem, view each illustration, to hear the artist's message. Then return again and again for entertainment, enlightenment, and inspiration.

Let the Morning Stars sing to you.

Suggested for Further Reading

Great Expectations by Charles Dickens

Heart of Darkness by Joseph Conrad

Anything by Edgar Allan Poe

Anything by William Shakespeare

ABOUT THE AUTHOR

RAY FOY writes about the current world situation and the consequential human dilemma, literary topics, book reviews, and inspirational themes. His fiction is mostly speculative with political and paranormal overtones.

You can follow Ray at his website: www.rayfoy.com.

And go to www.arbordinparkpress.net or www.amazon.com to find Ray's collection of short fiction:

The Wider World

www.ingramcontent.com/pod-product-compliance
Lightning Source LLC
Chambersburg PA
CBHW031346040426
42444CB00005B/208